Also by the author:

NOVELS:

Life is But a Dream: On The Lake
Life is But a Dream: In The Mountains
Broken Resolutions
Cooper Moon: The Calling
Cooper Moon: The Temptation
Cooper Moon: The Fall
Cooper Moon: The Grace

BOOKS FOR CHILDREN:

Let's Learn About Dogs
Let's Learn About Cats
Let's Learn About Things to Drive
Let's Learn About Jungle Animals
Let's Learn About Birds
Let's Learn About Wild Animals
Let's Learn About Horse
Let's Learn About Farm Animals
I Love You When (For Girls)
I Love You When (For Boys)

NON-FICTION:

You Don't Need a Prince: A Letter to My Daughter
What's Your Story: Icebreaker Questions for Small Groups
Character Profile: Make Your Characters Come to Life
Heart Breathings: Writing Prompts to Inspire and Ignite Your Fiction

COLORING BOOKS FOR ADULTS:

Go to **2old2color.com** for available titles

Adult Coloring Books

2 Old 2 Color

Flowers

CHERYL SHIREMAN

DEDICATION

To Noah Carter Benjamin – our beloved first grandson.
Adorable, adventurous, and too many miles away.

Are you ready to have some fun?

Thank you for buying this volume of the 2 Old 2 Color series.

Release your inner child with this coloring book for adults! Forty fun and creative original images for endless hours of coloring bliss. After a few hours of coloring you may find yourself chewing bubble gum and wishing on stars. Don't say we didn't warn you.

Although all of our images are printed on one side of the page for easy coloring, we highly recommend inserting a blank sheet of paper in between the images before coloring to prevent any possible bleed through.

CAUTION: Use of this product may result in an increase in joy, spontaneous giggling, and the urge to run through mud puddles.

Now – let the coloring begin!

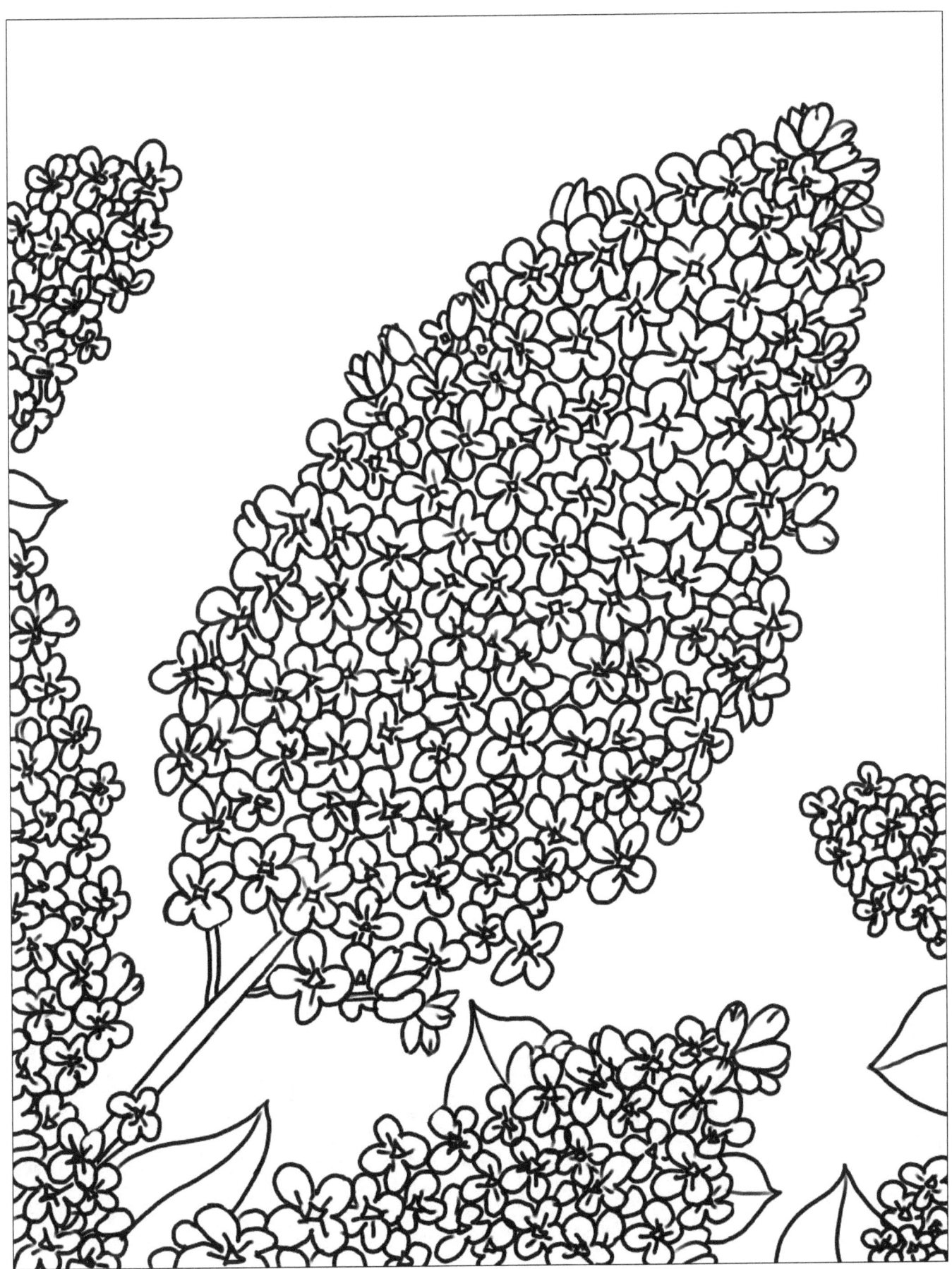

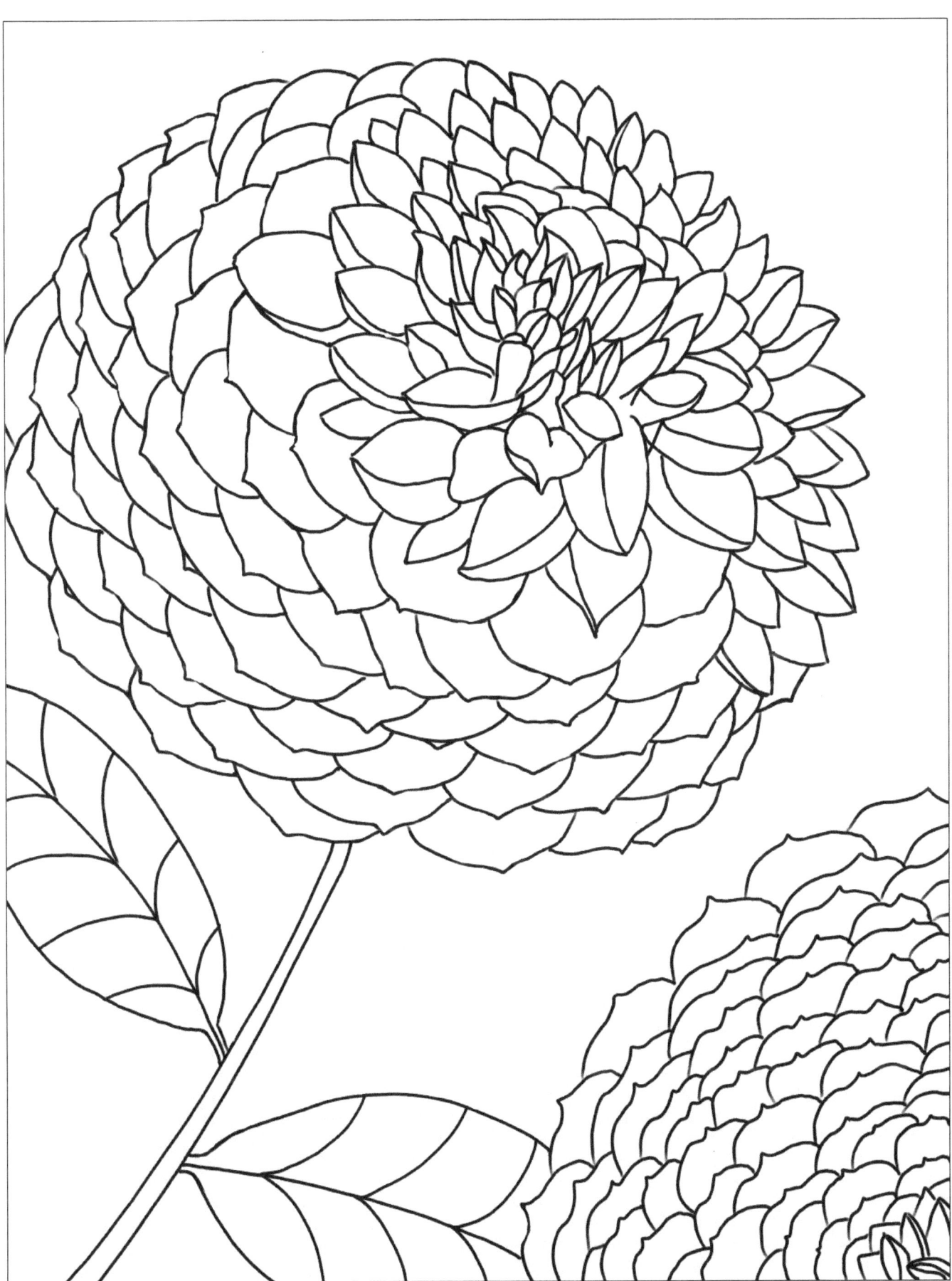

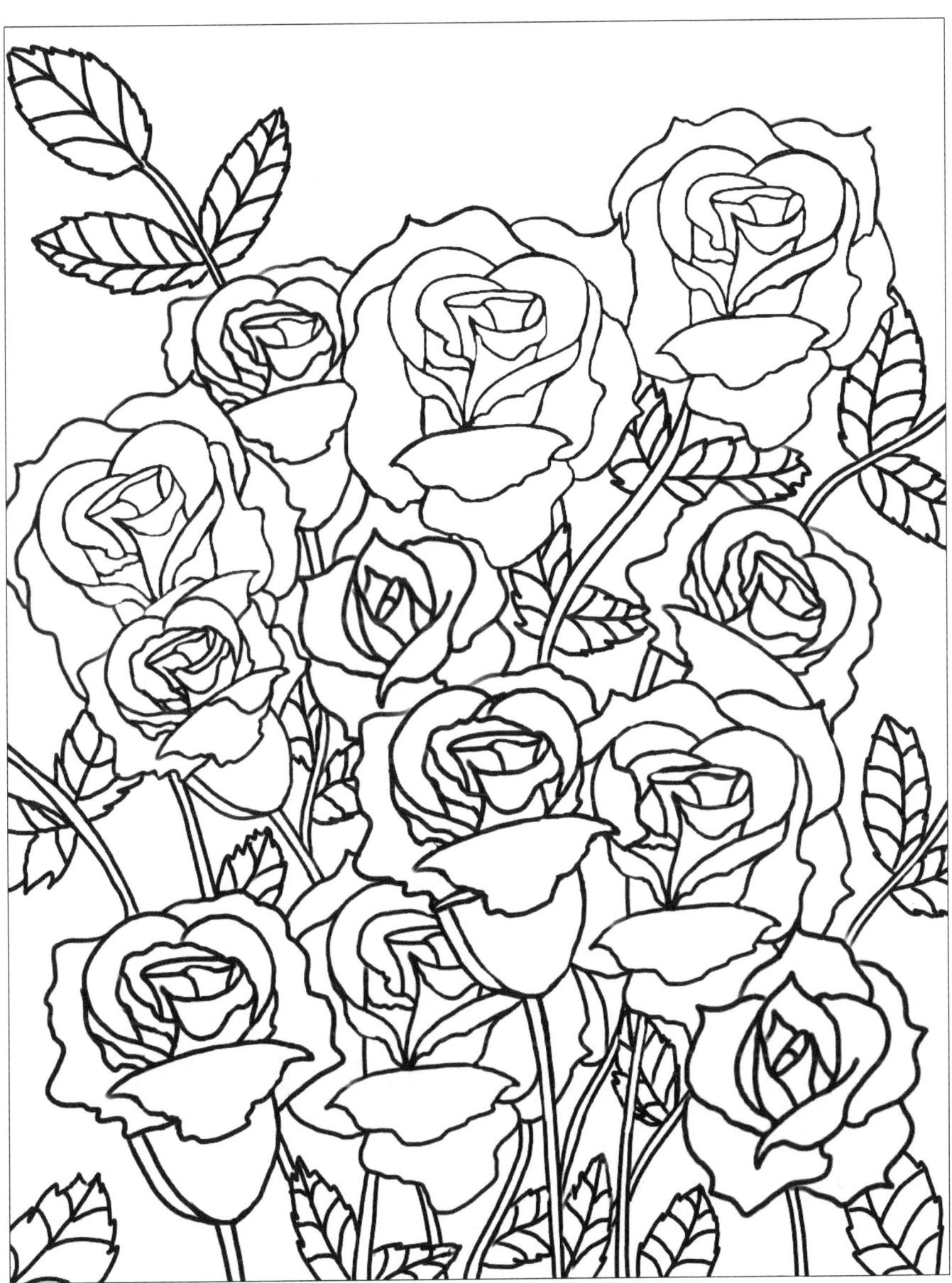

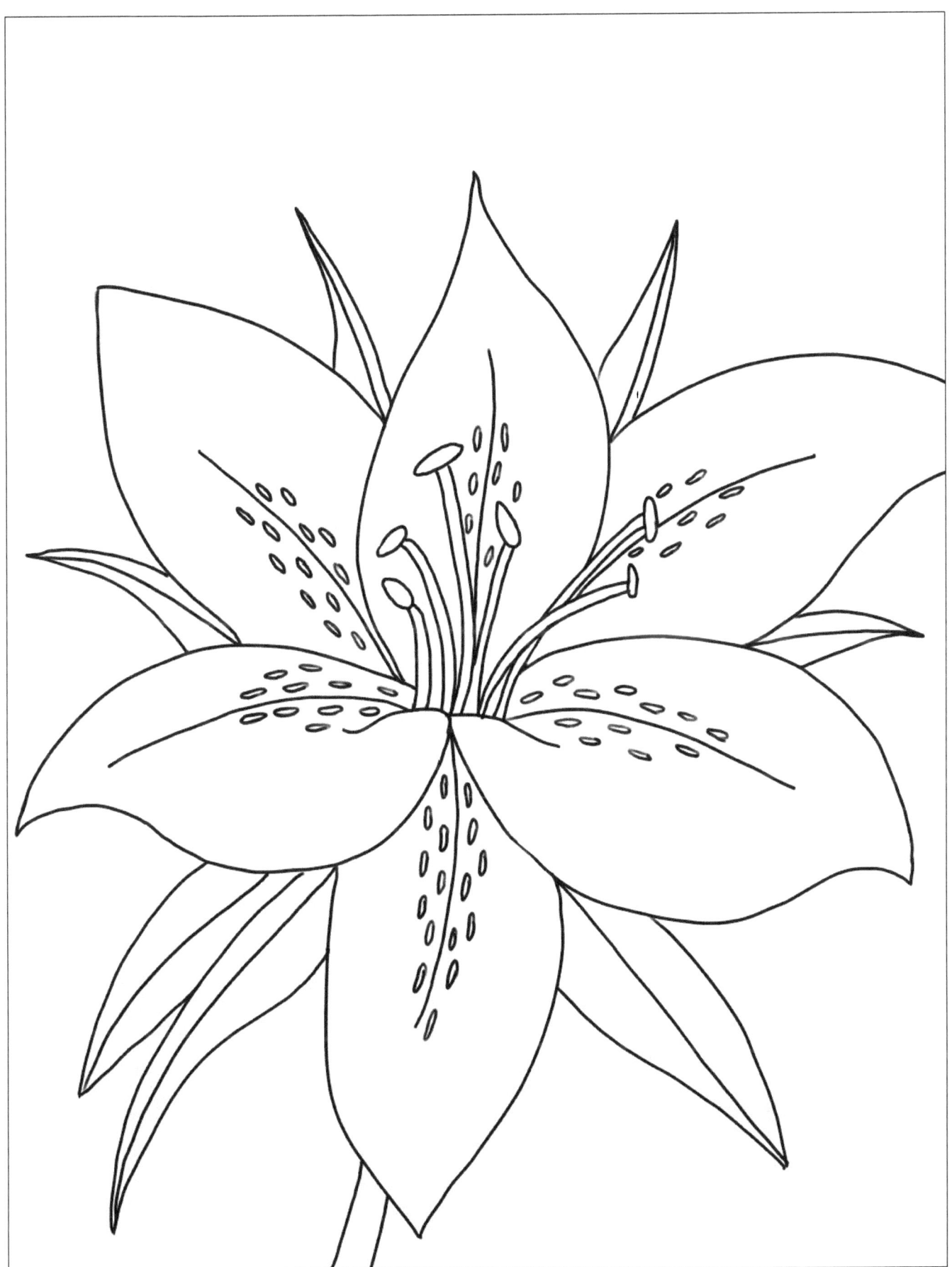

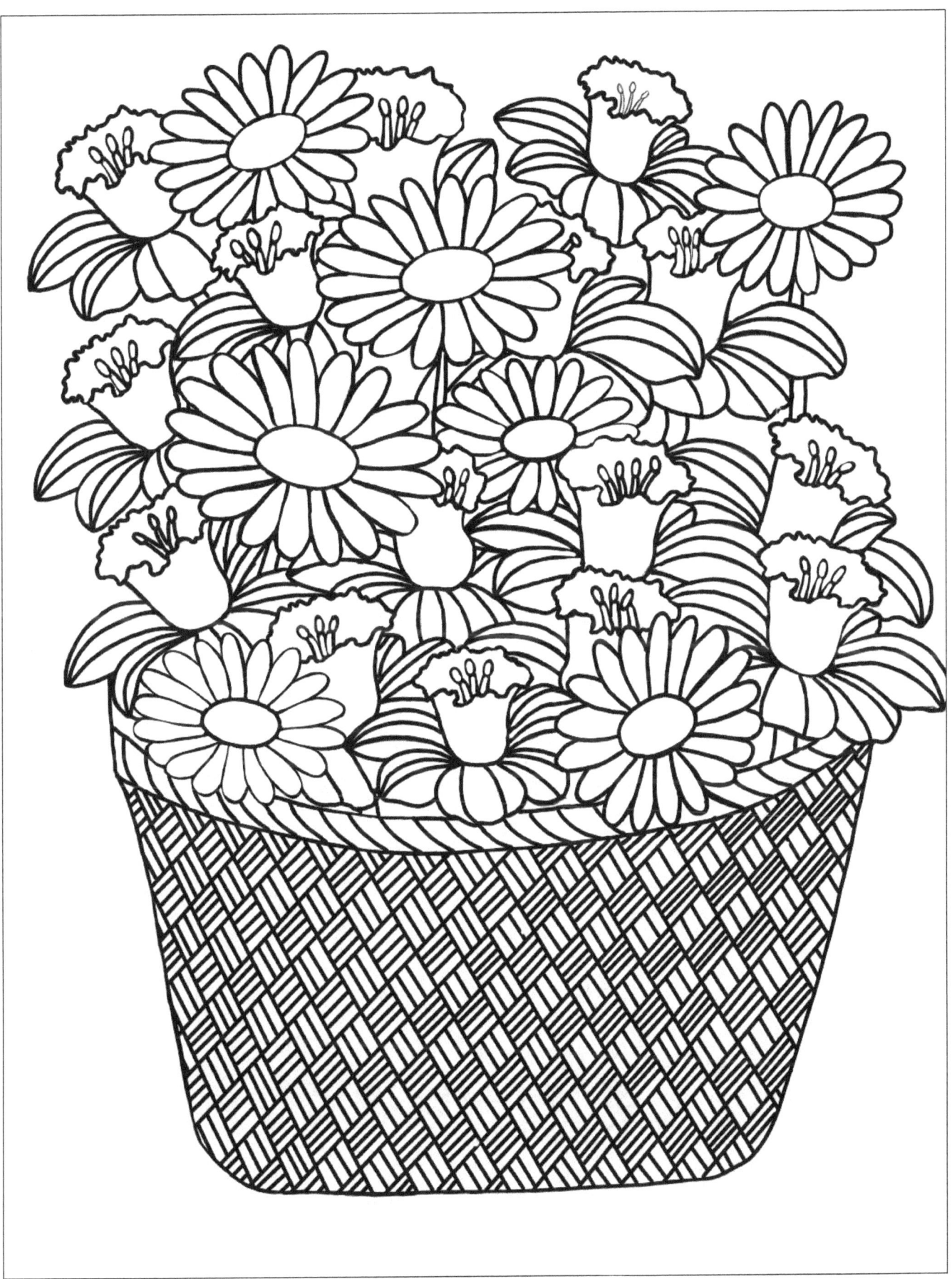

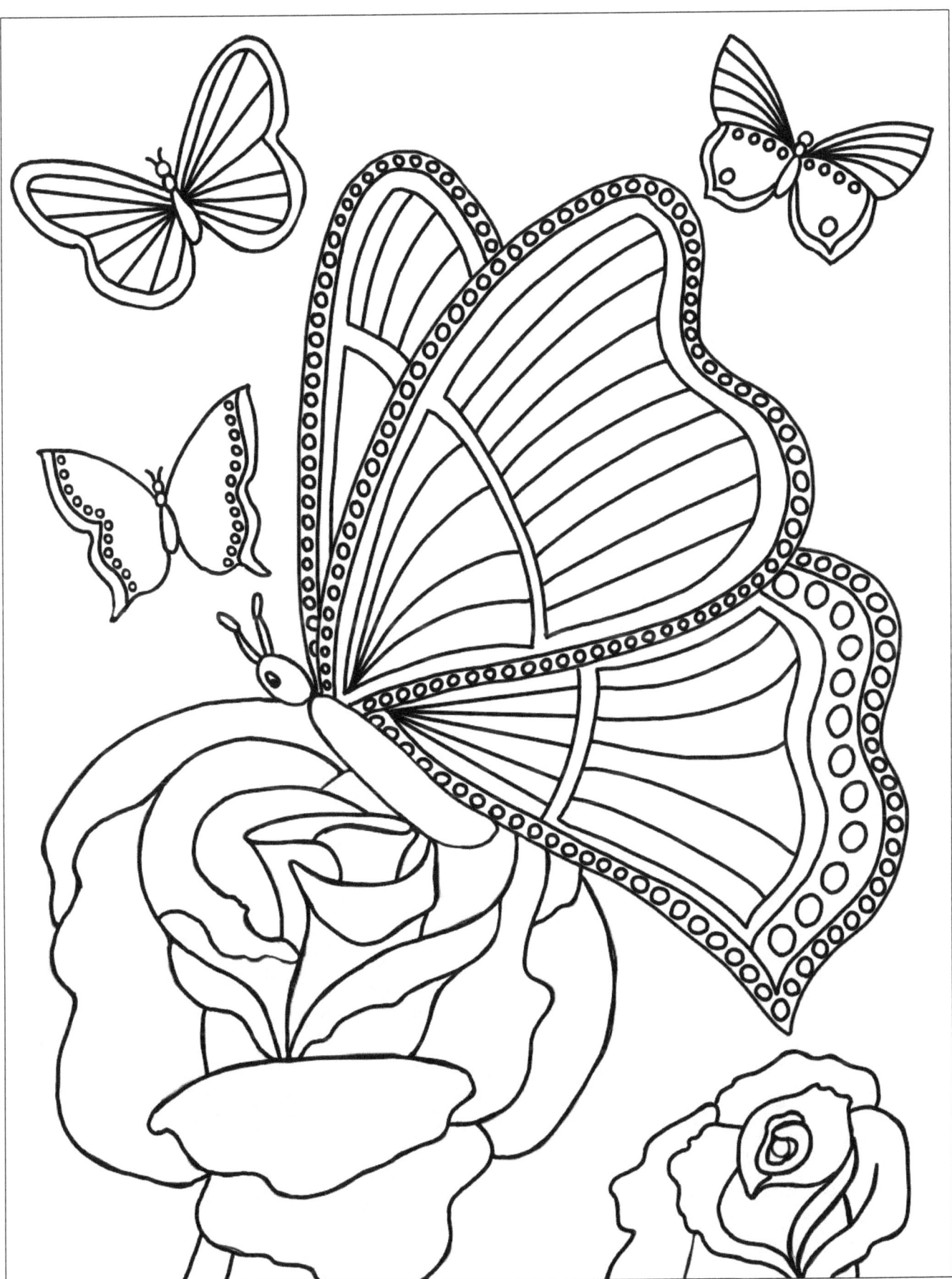

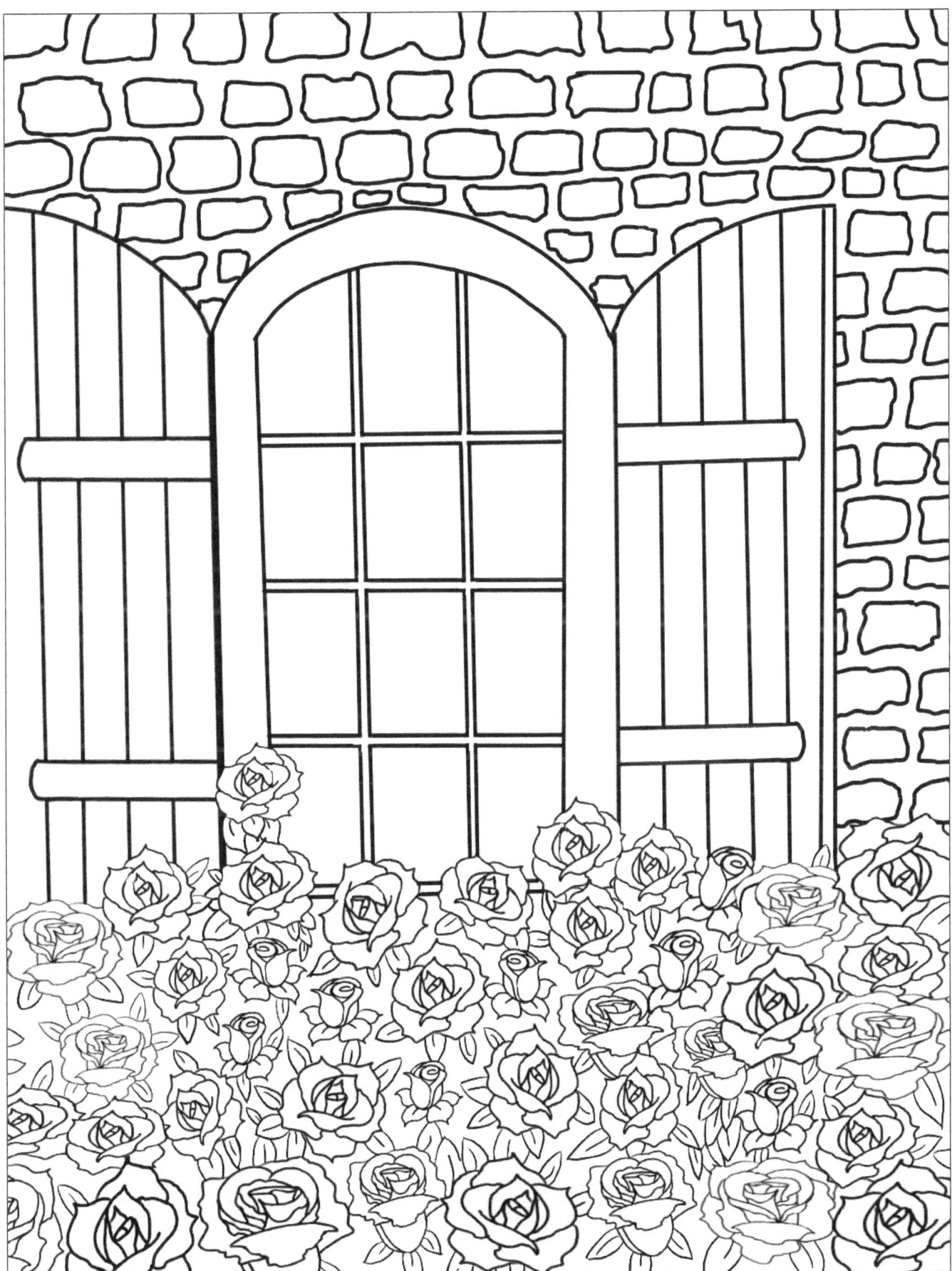

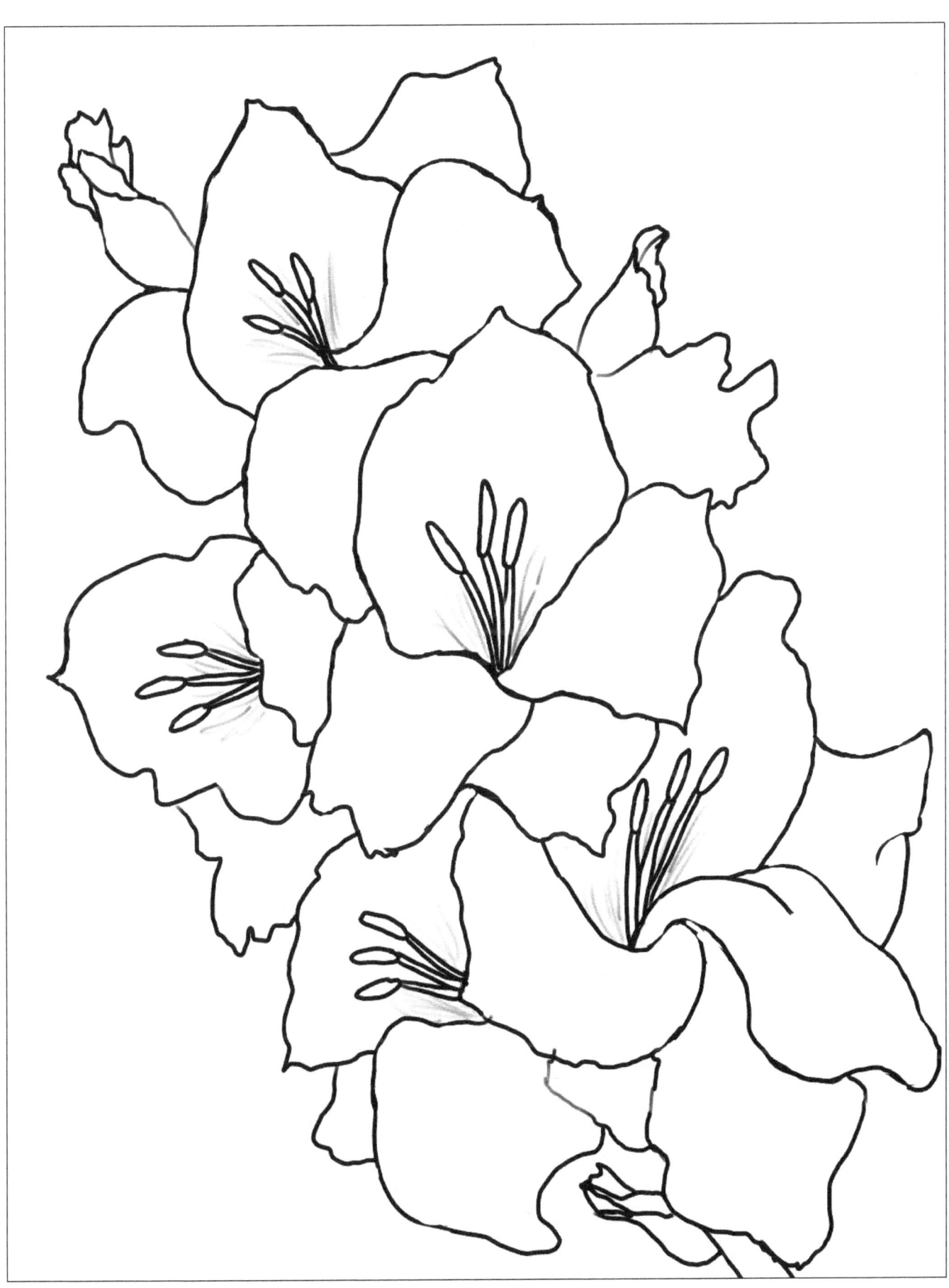

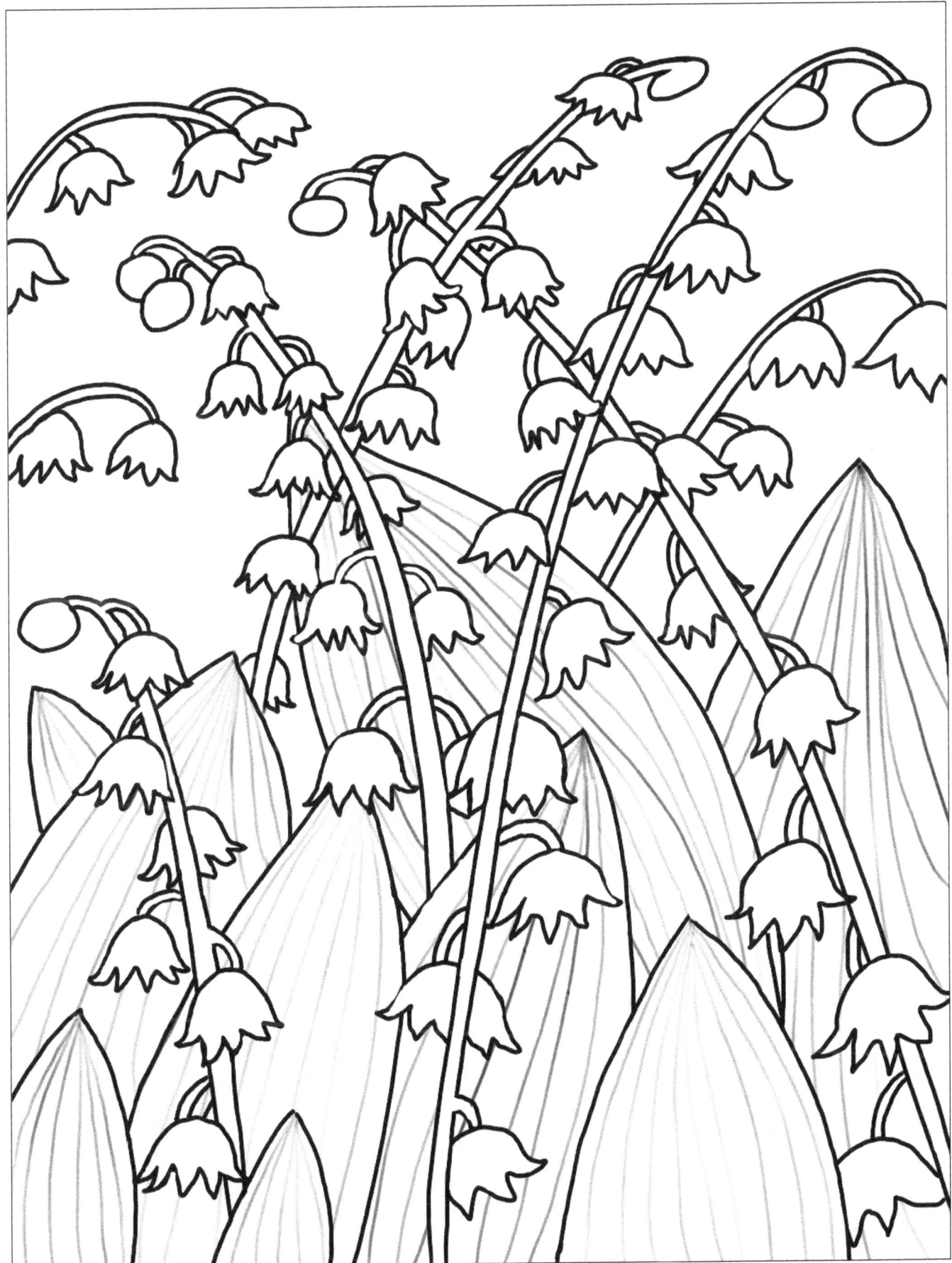

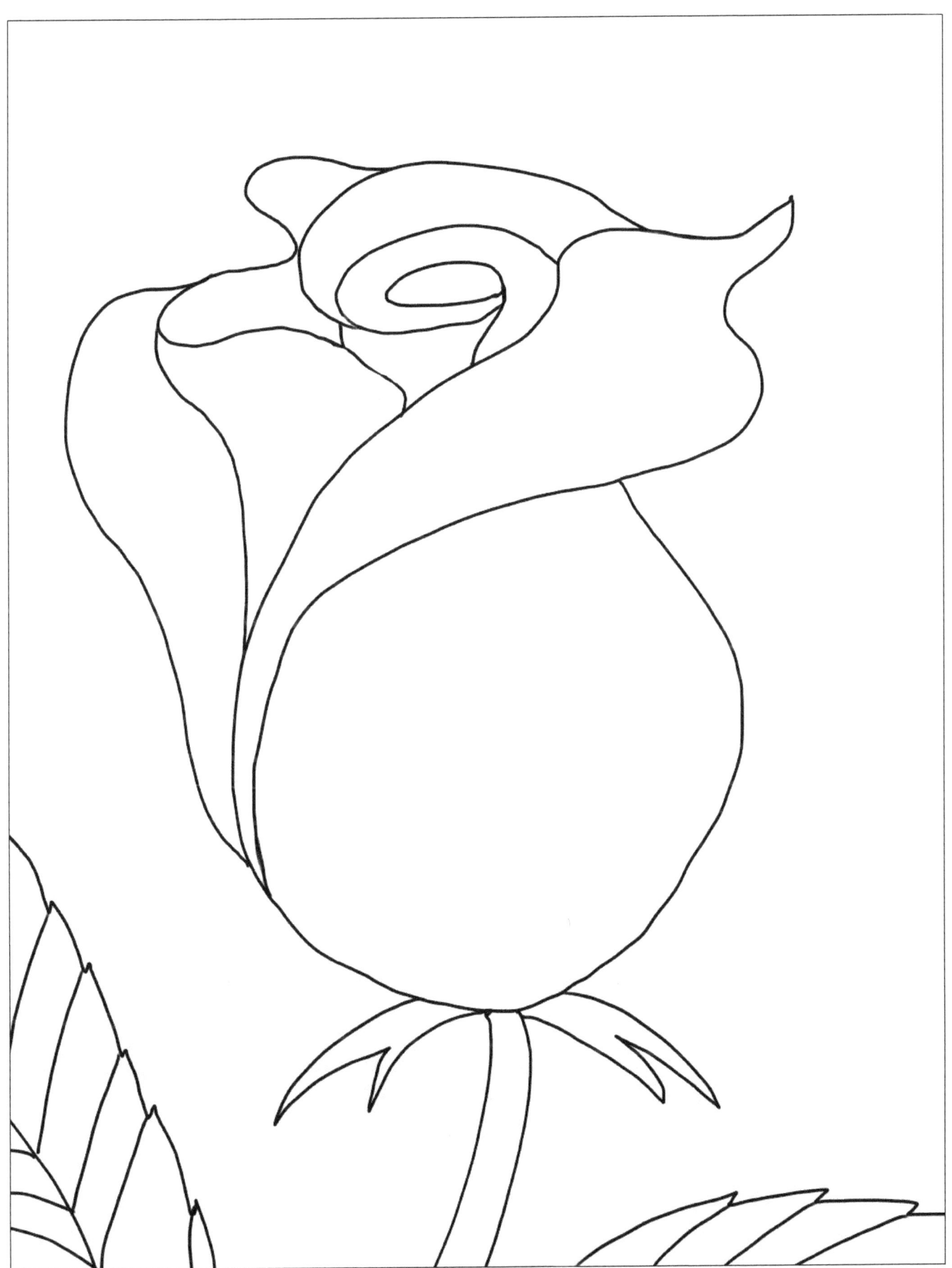

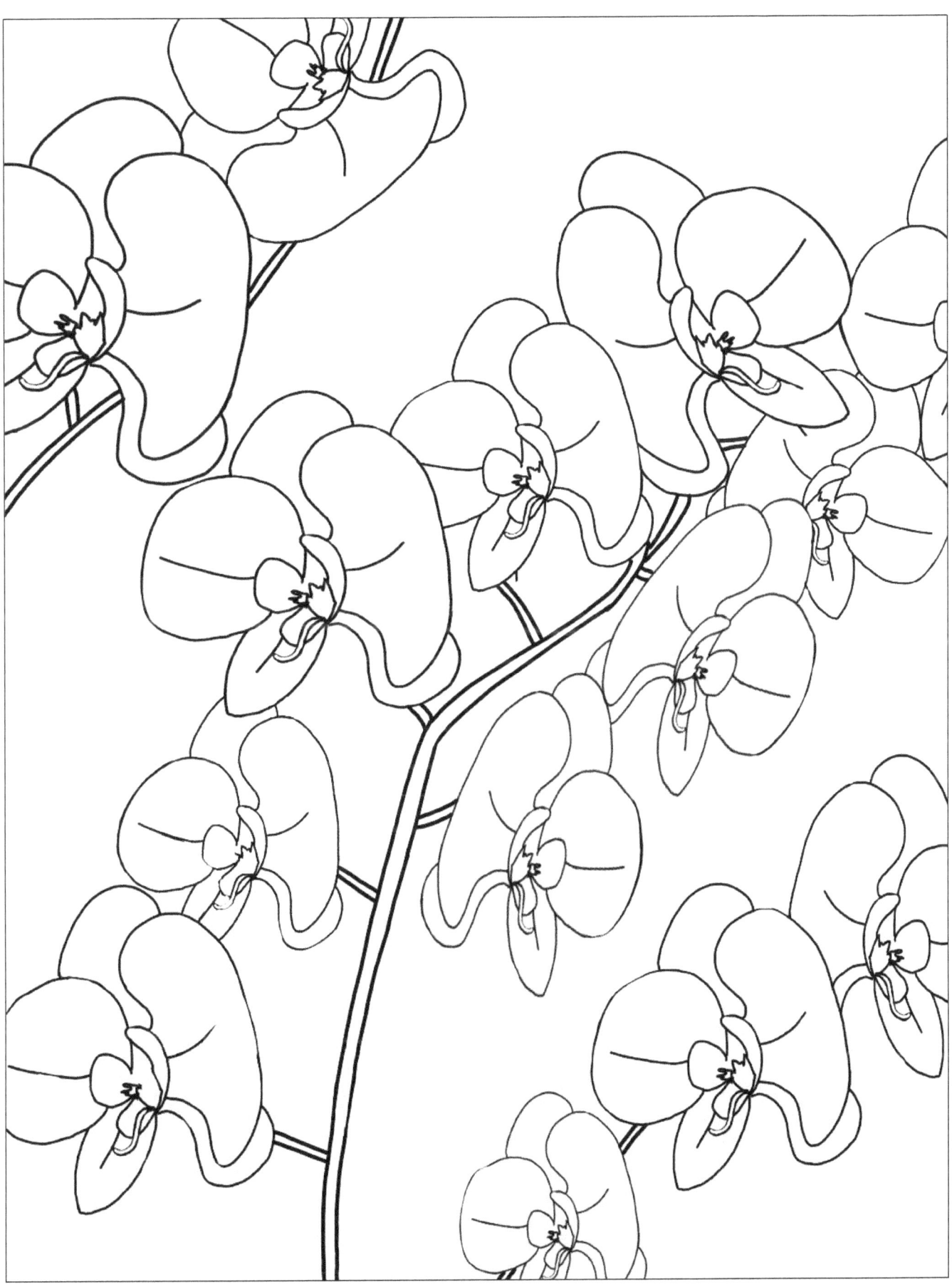

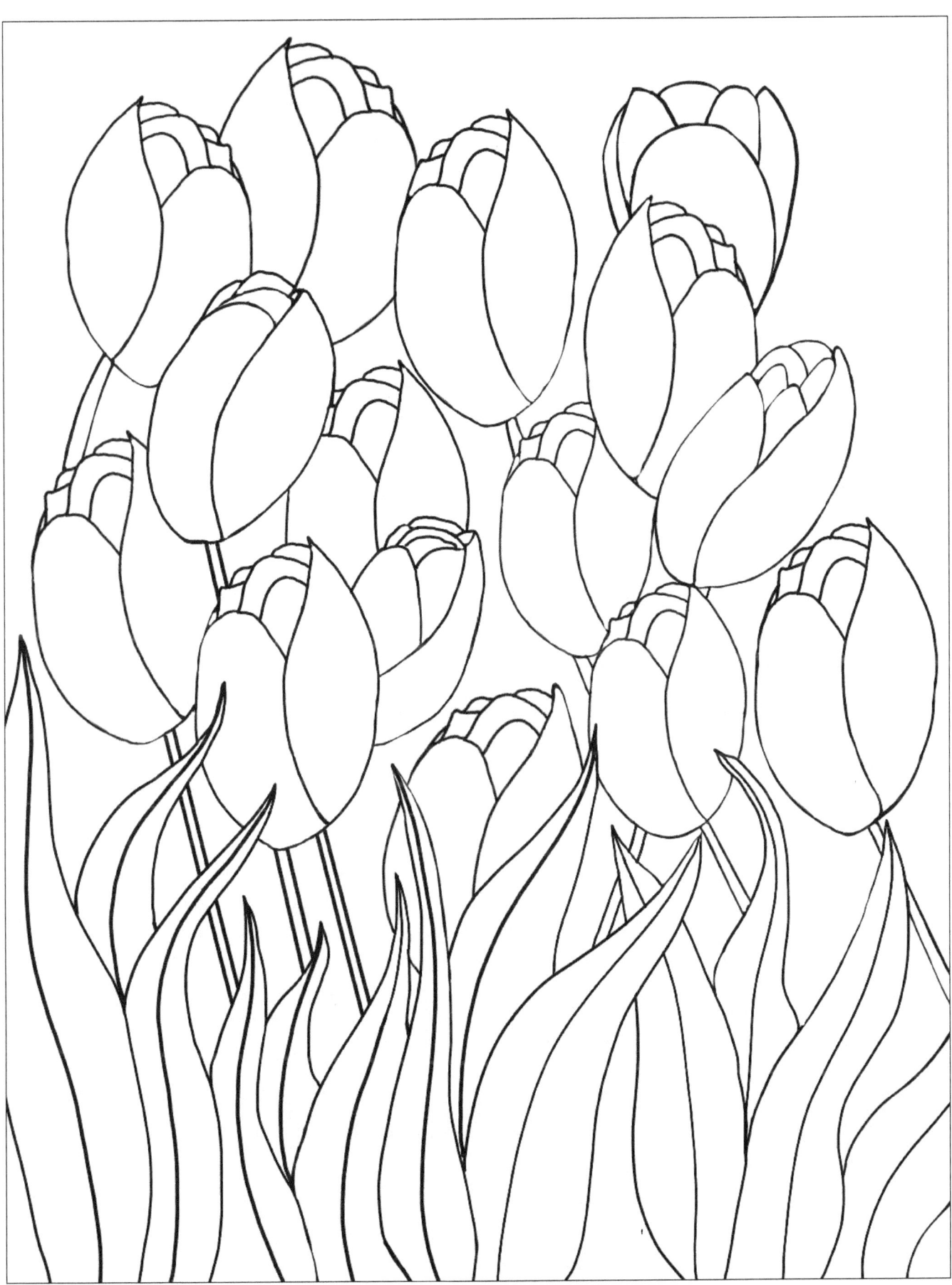

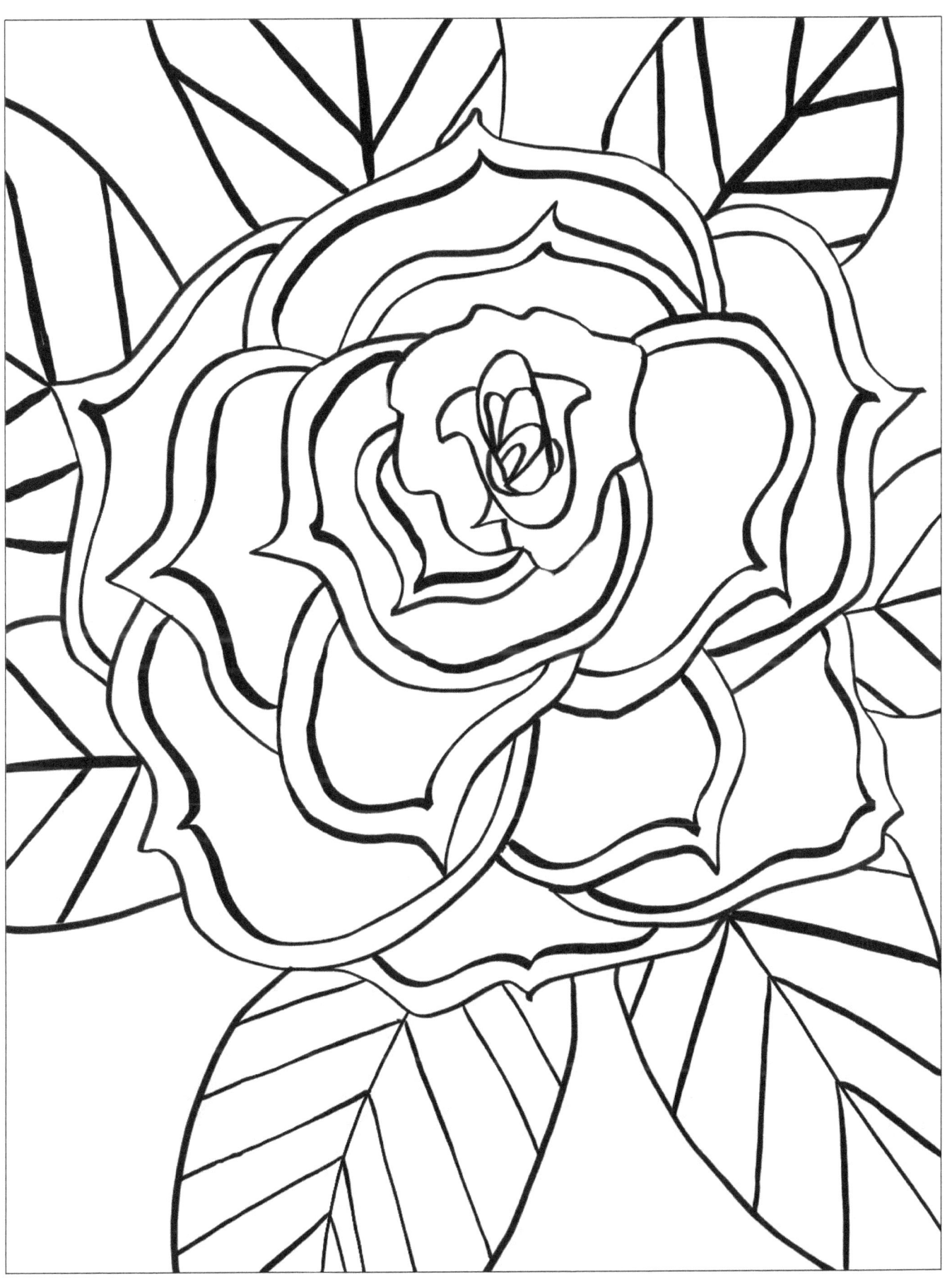

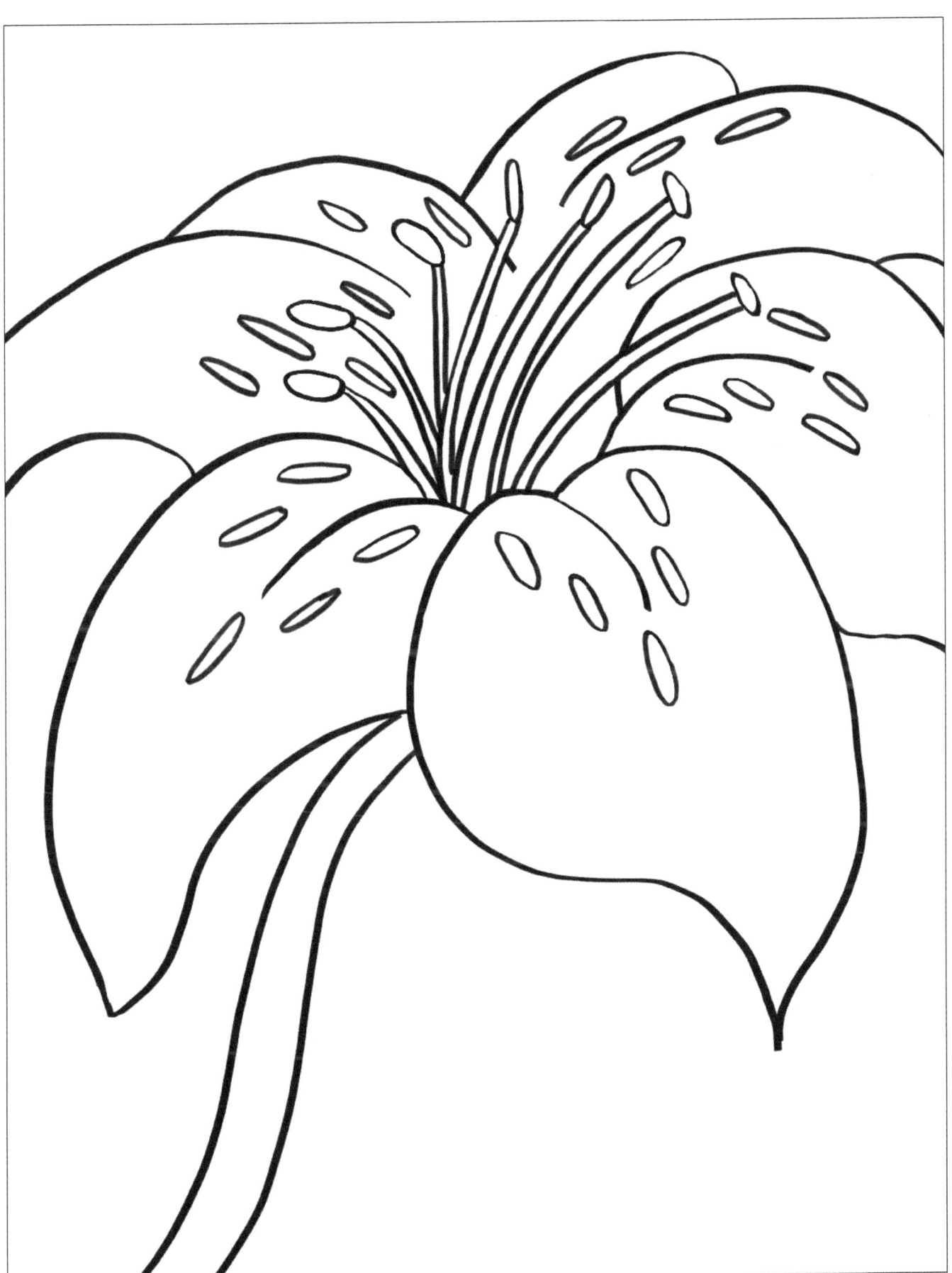

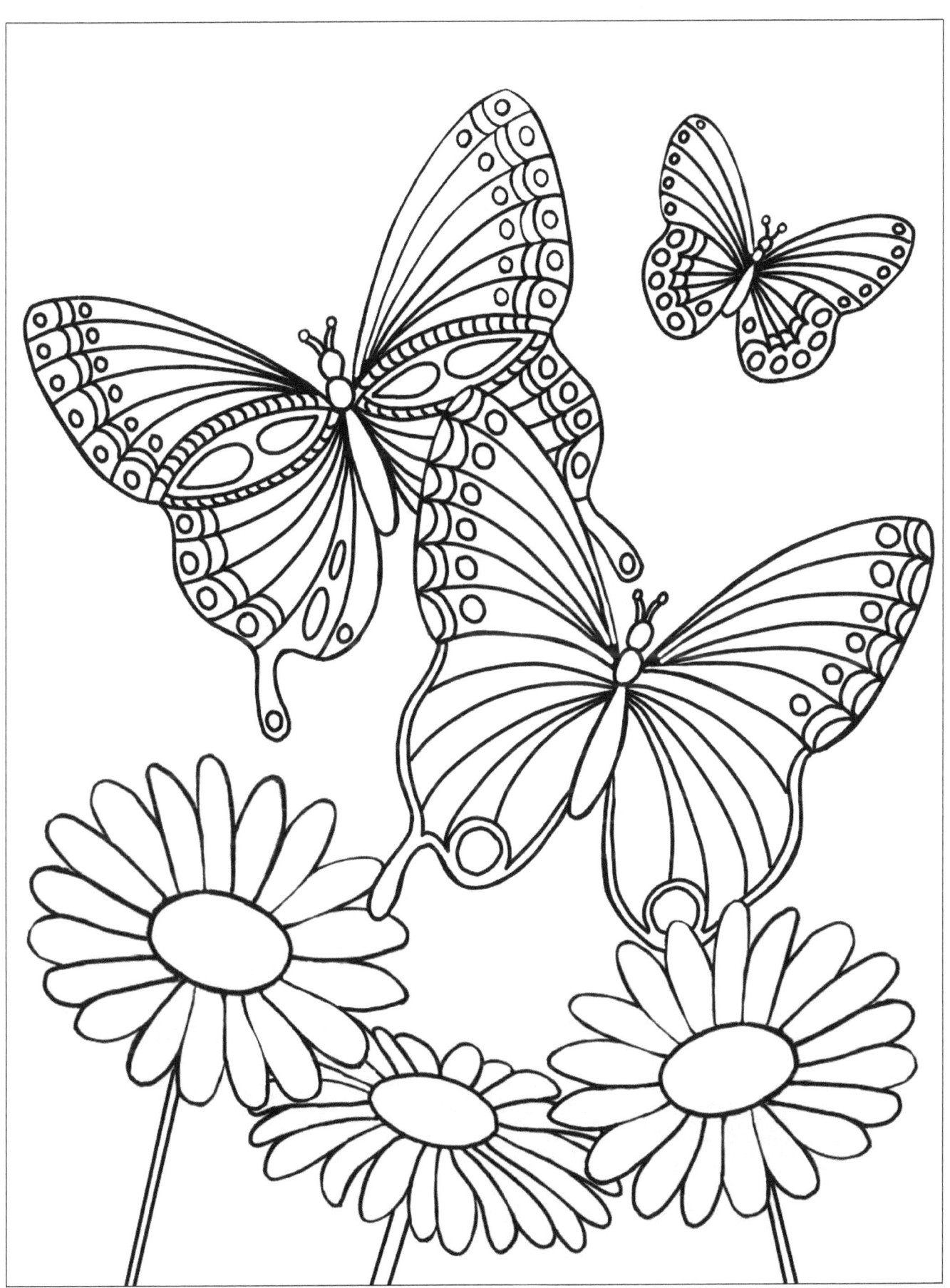

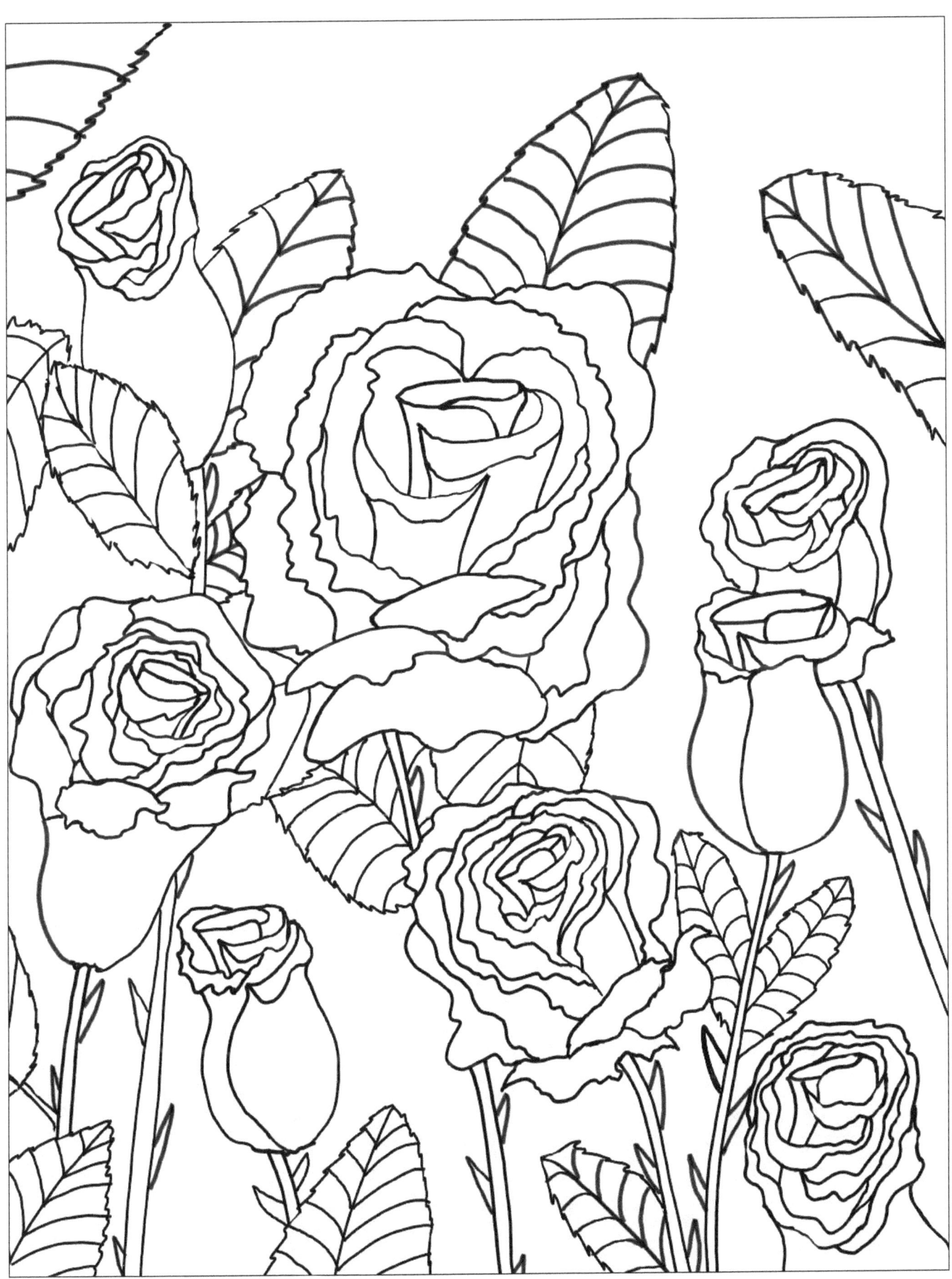

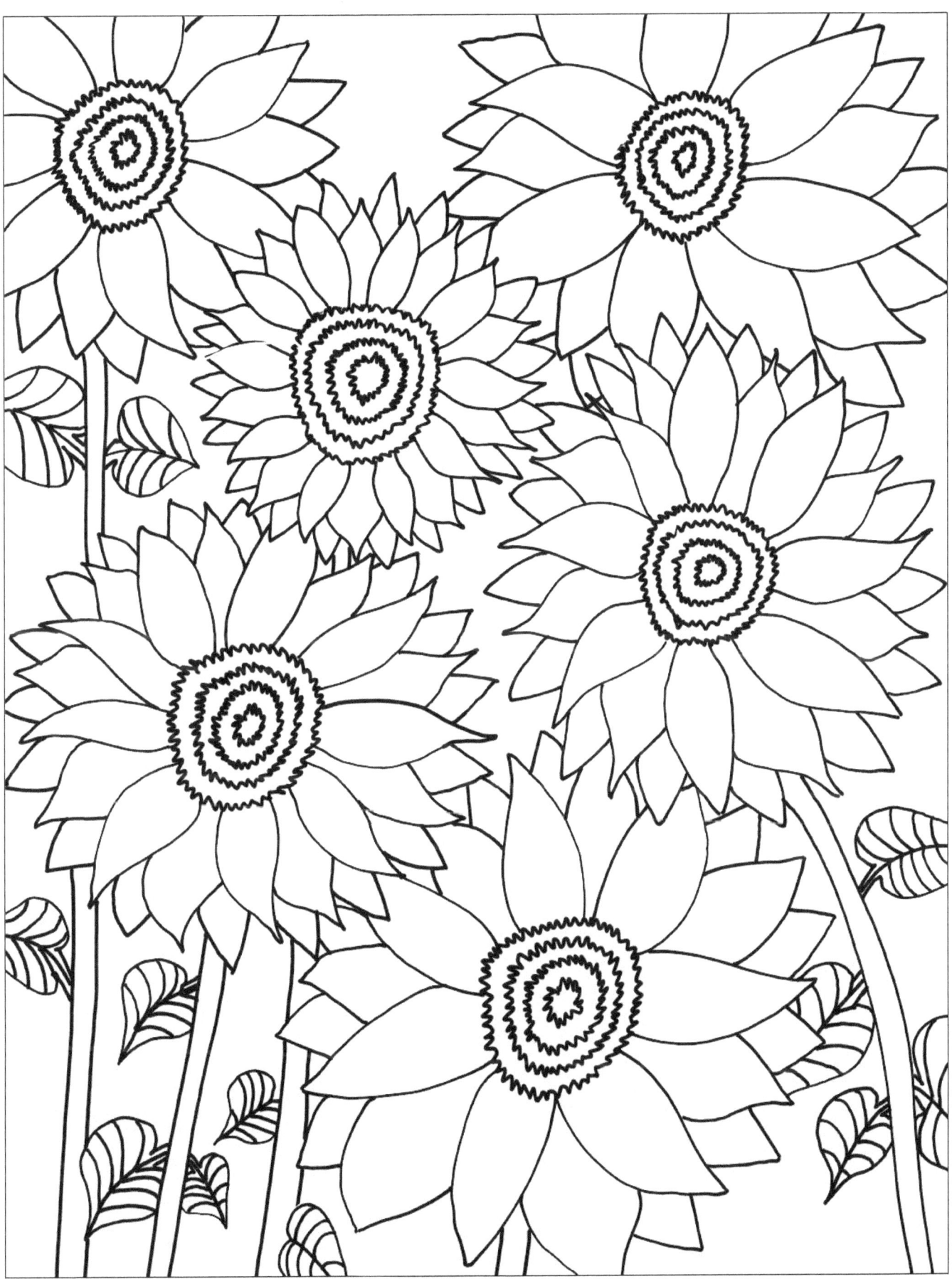

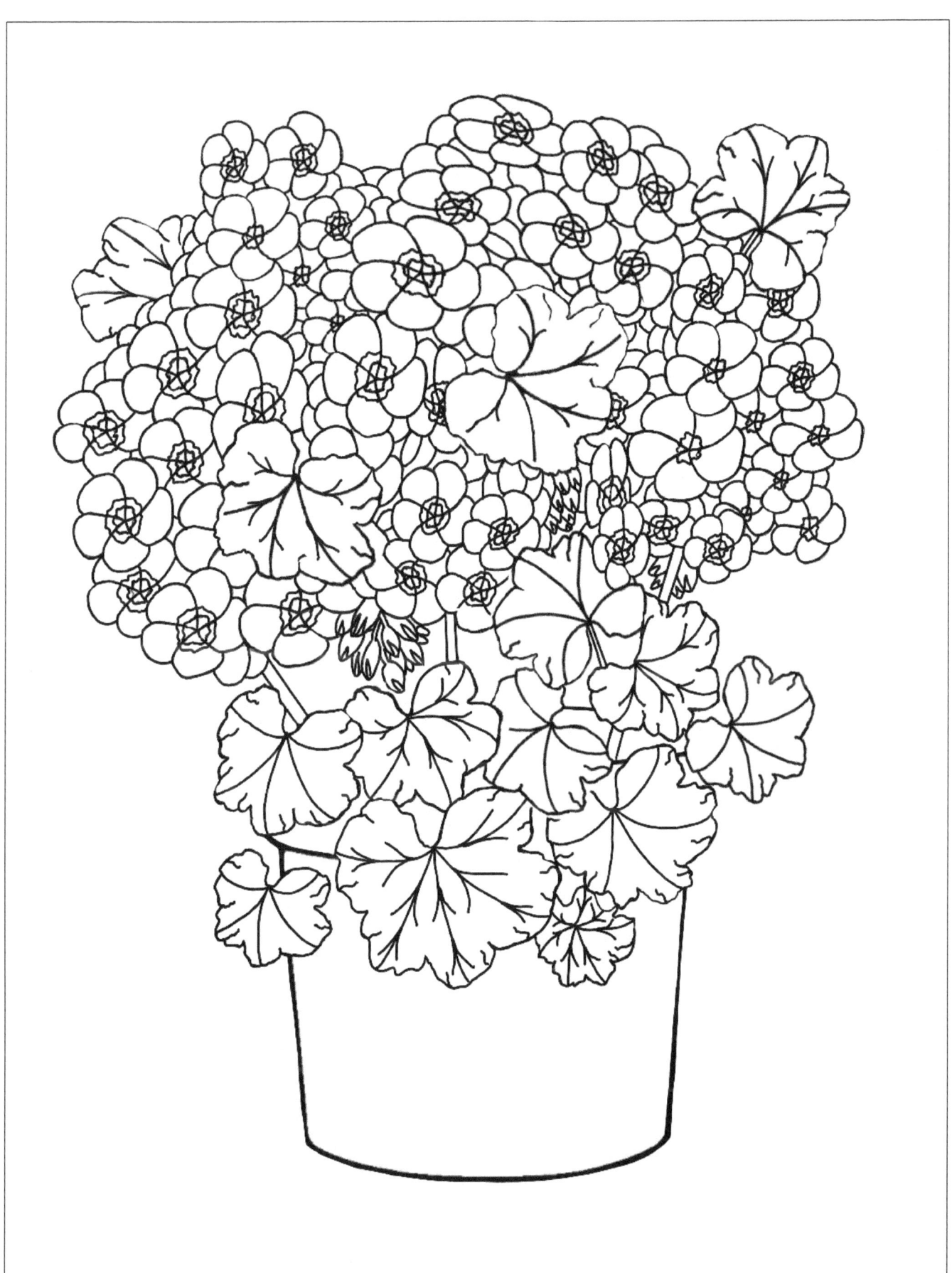

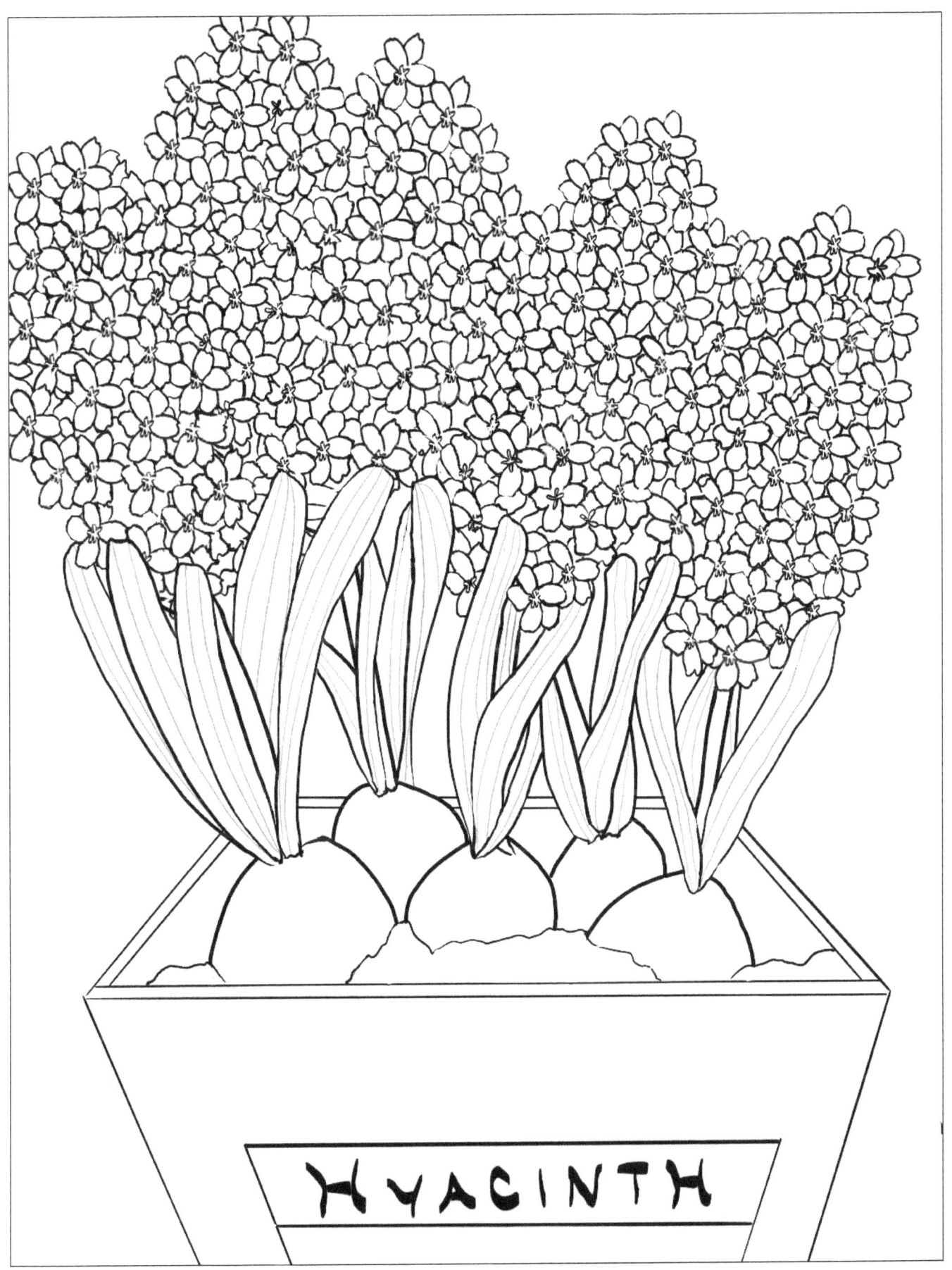

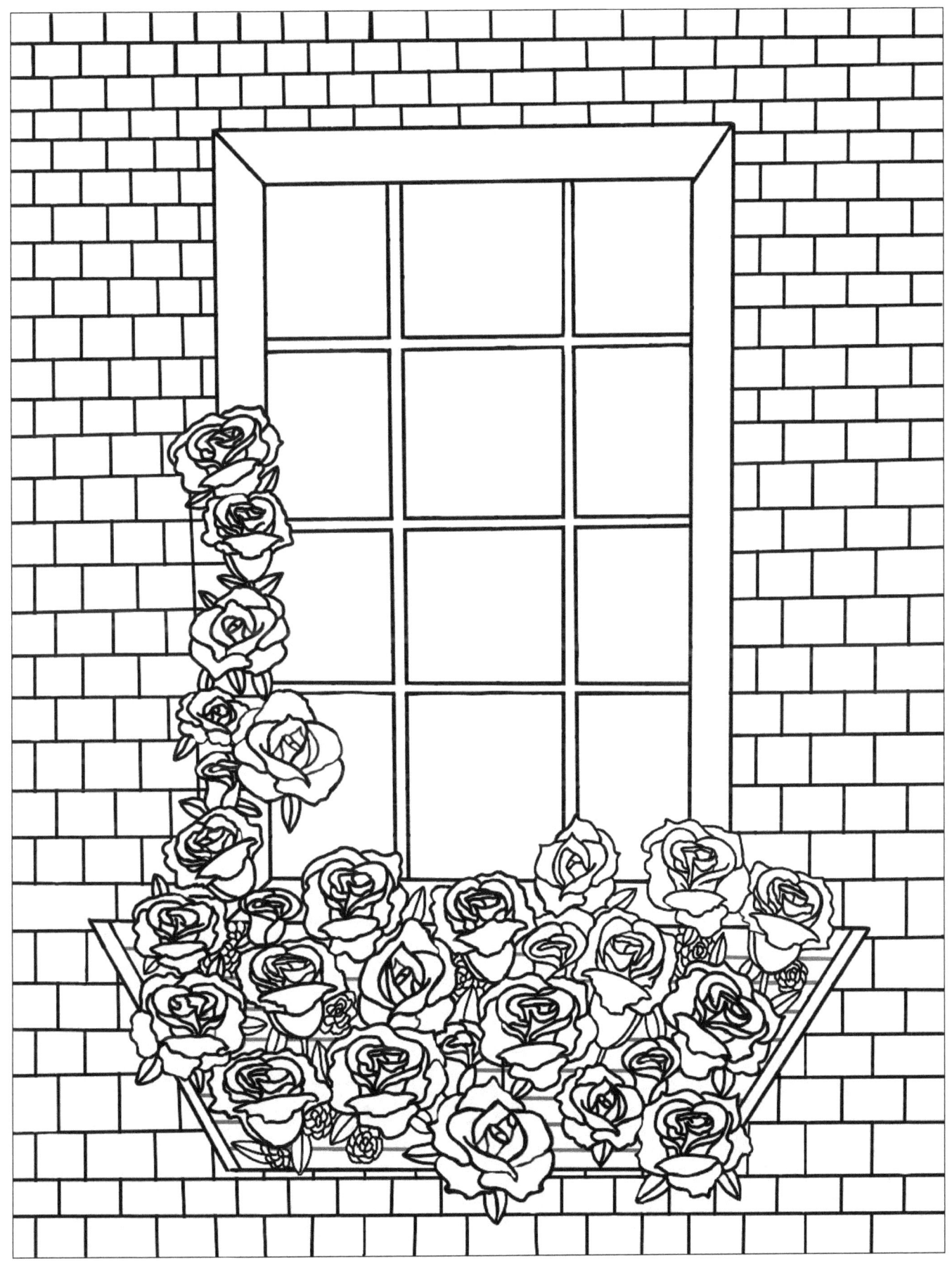

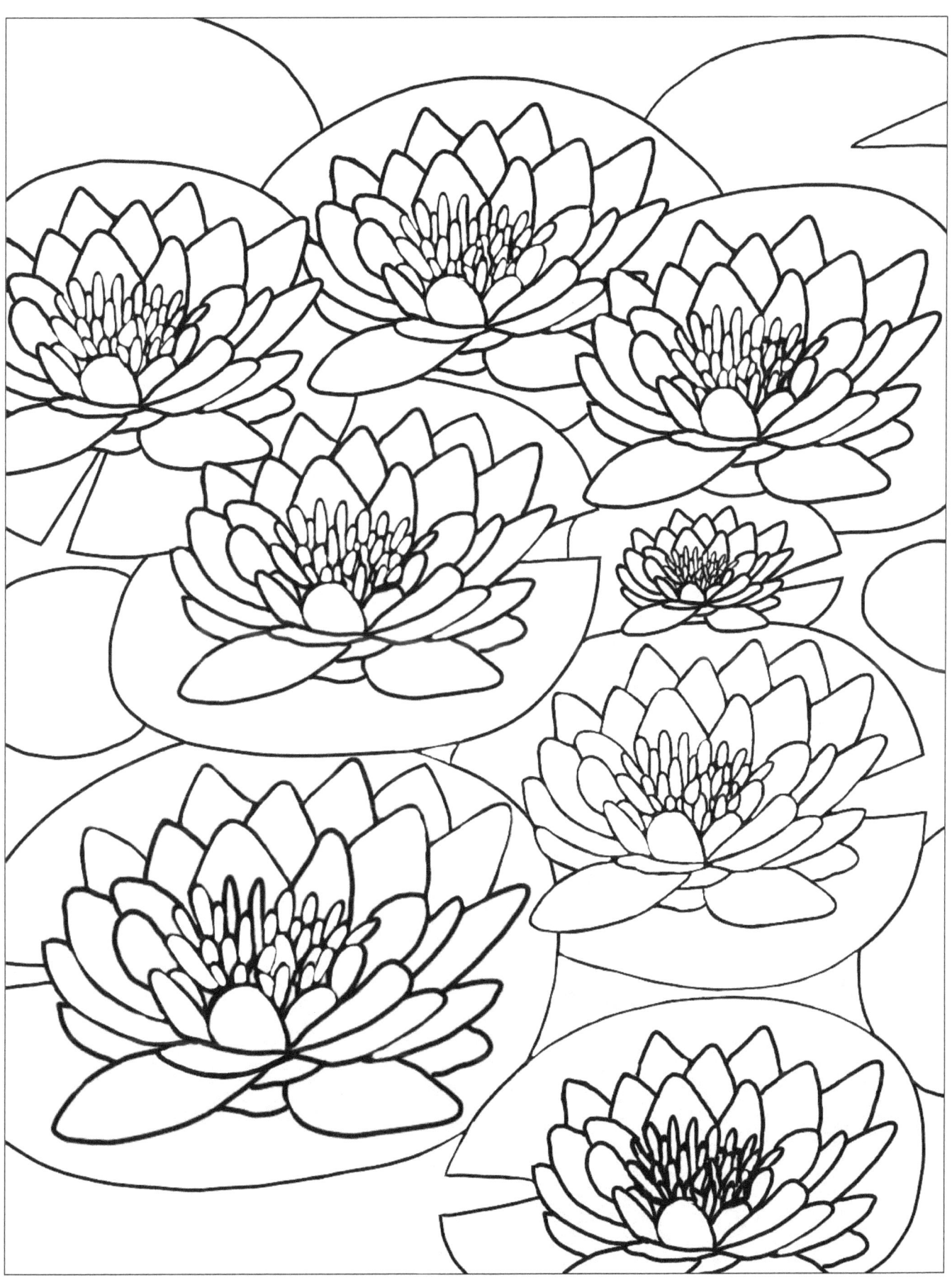

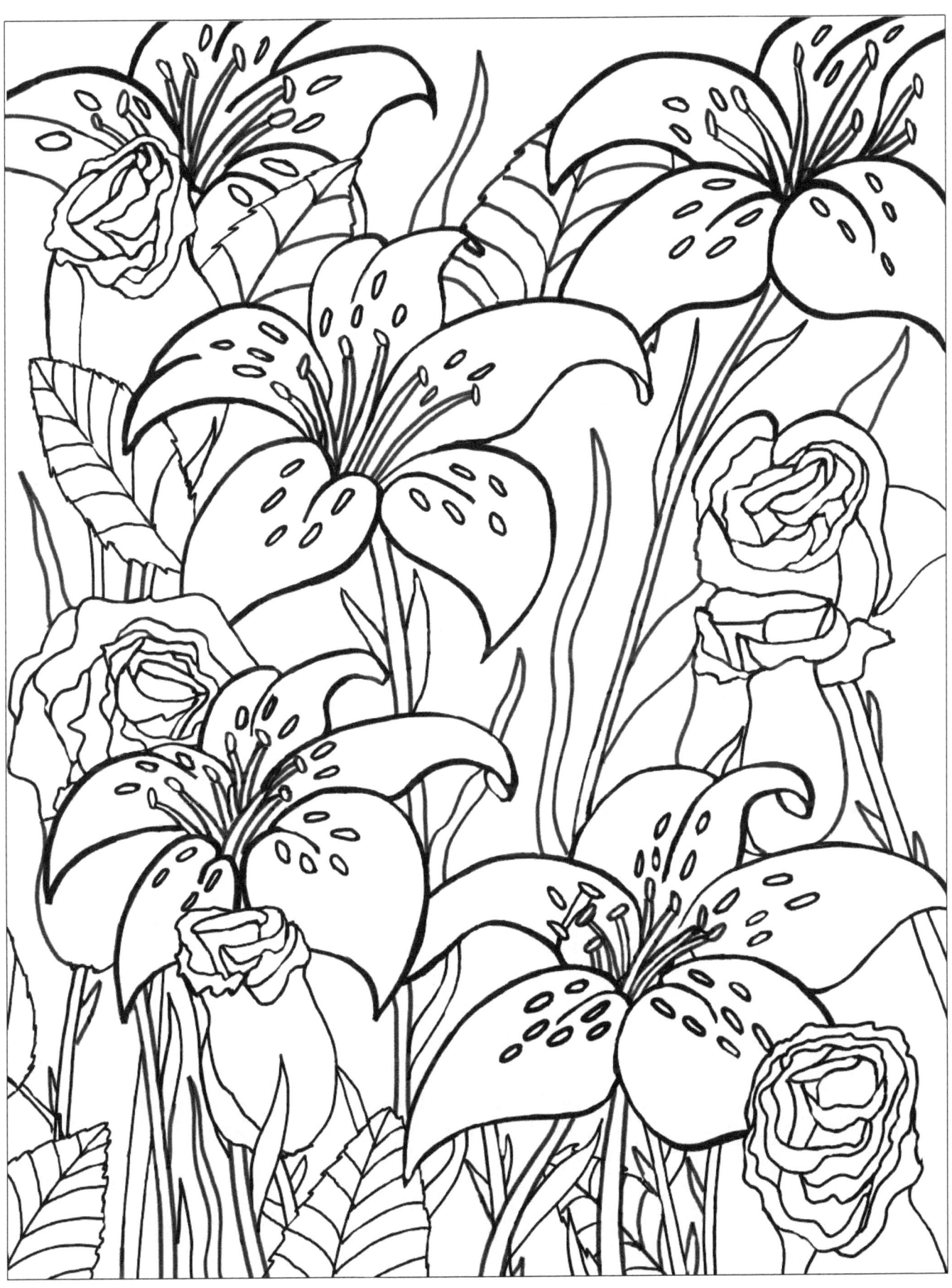

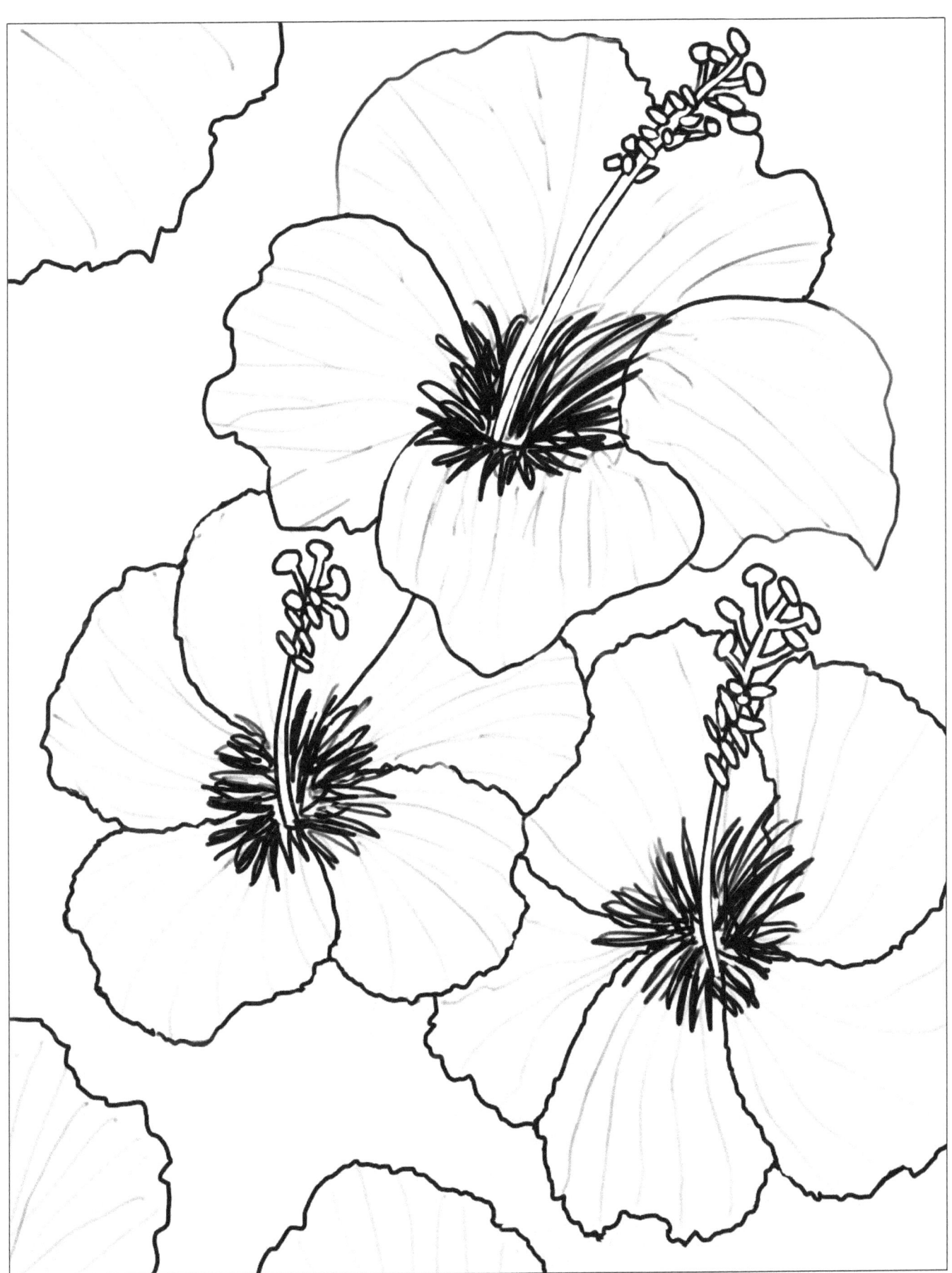

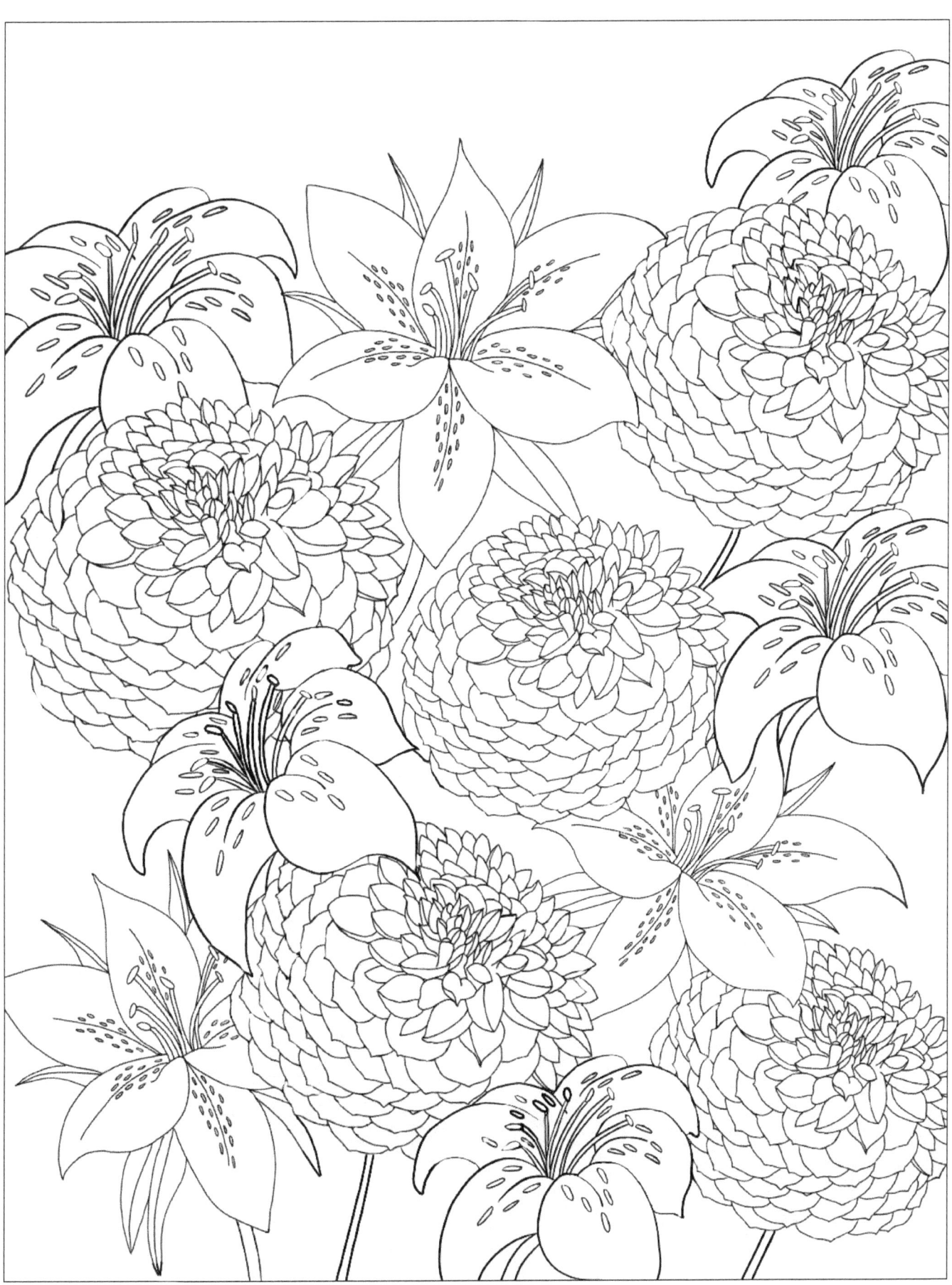

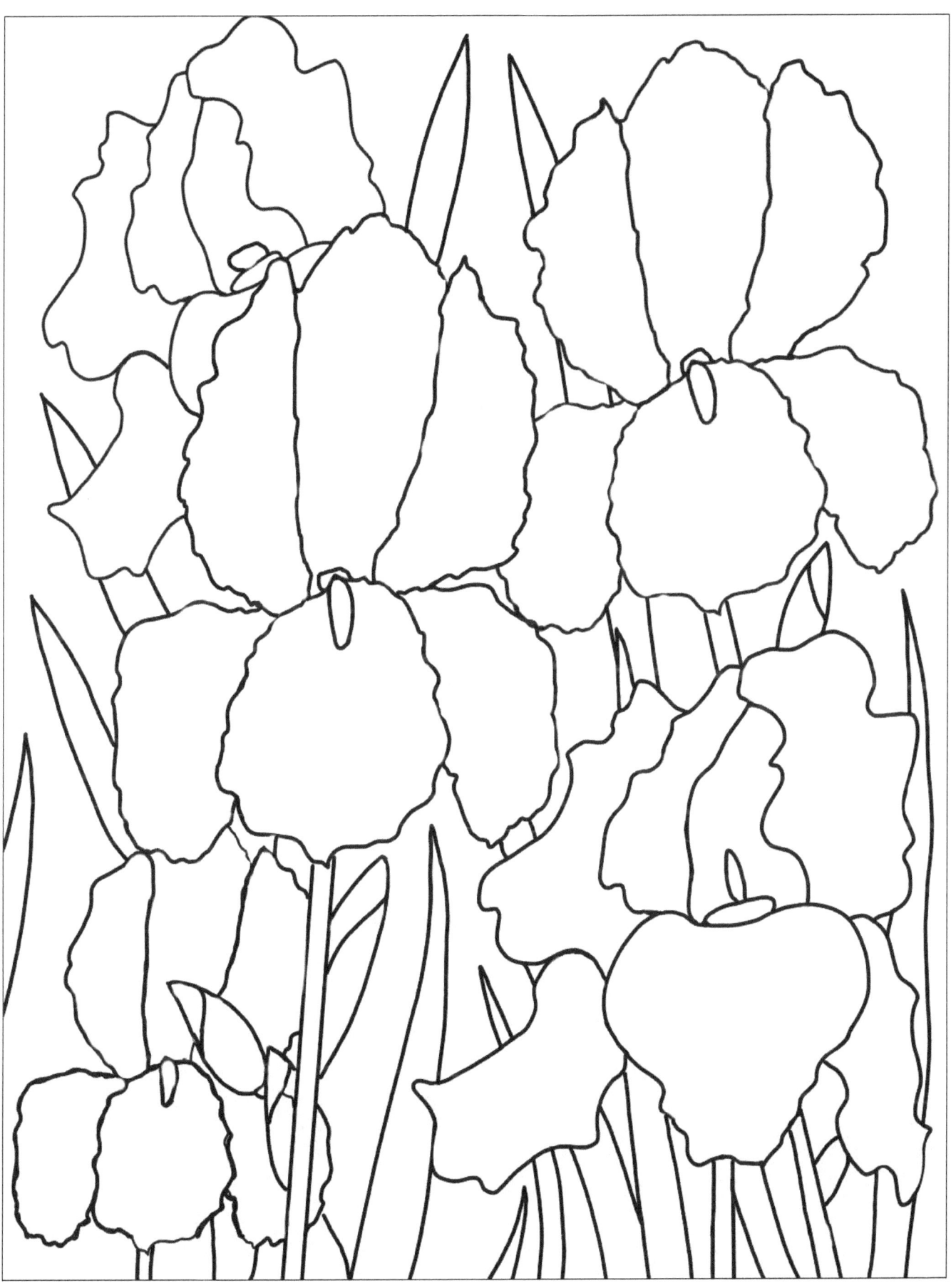

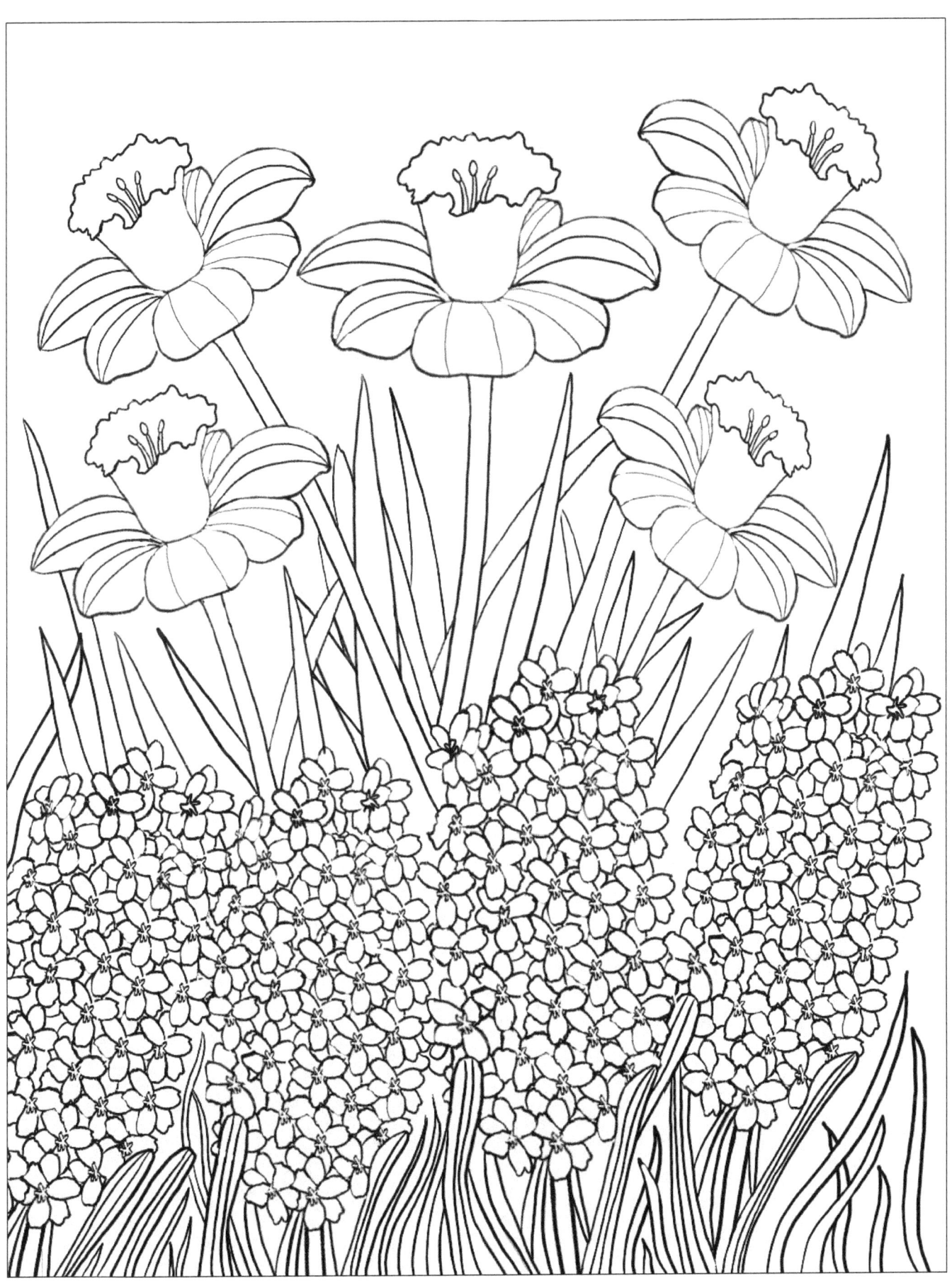

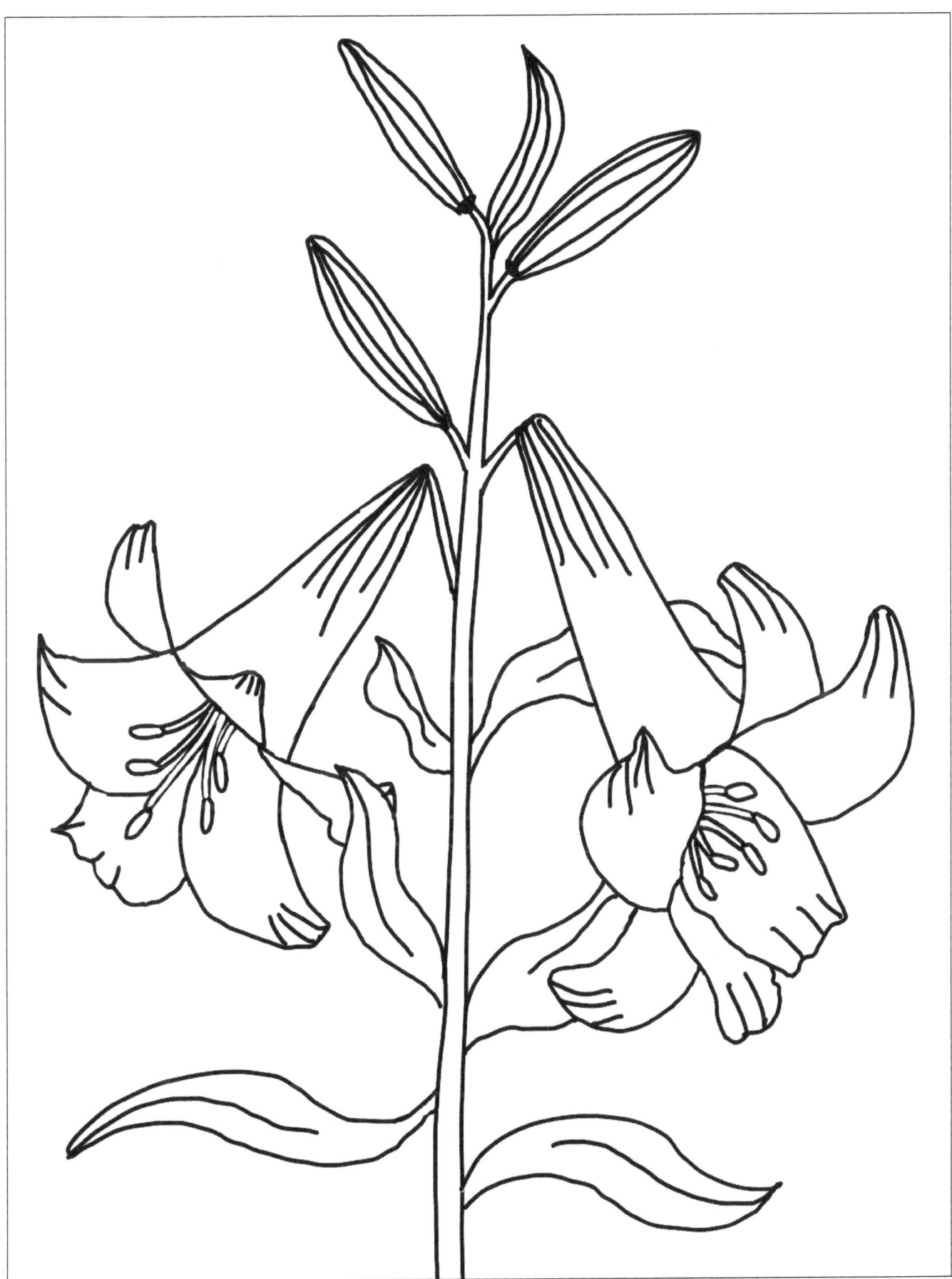

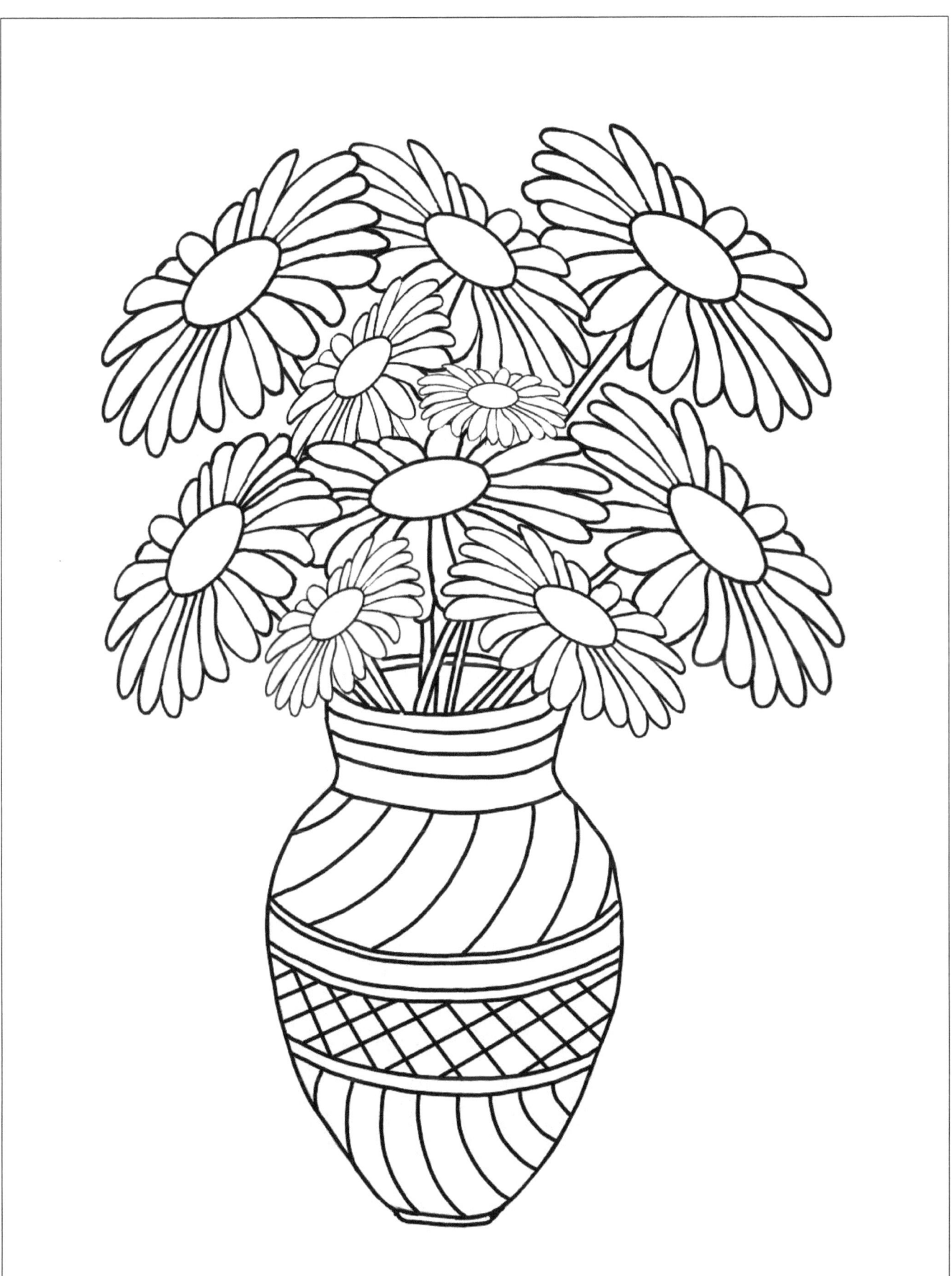

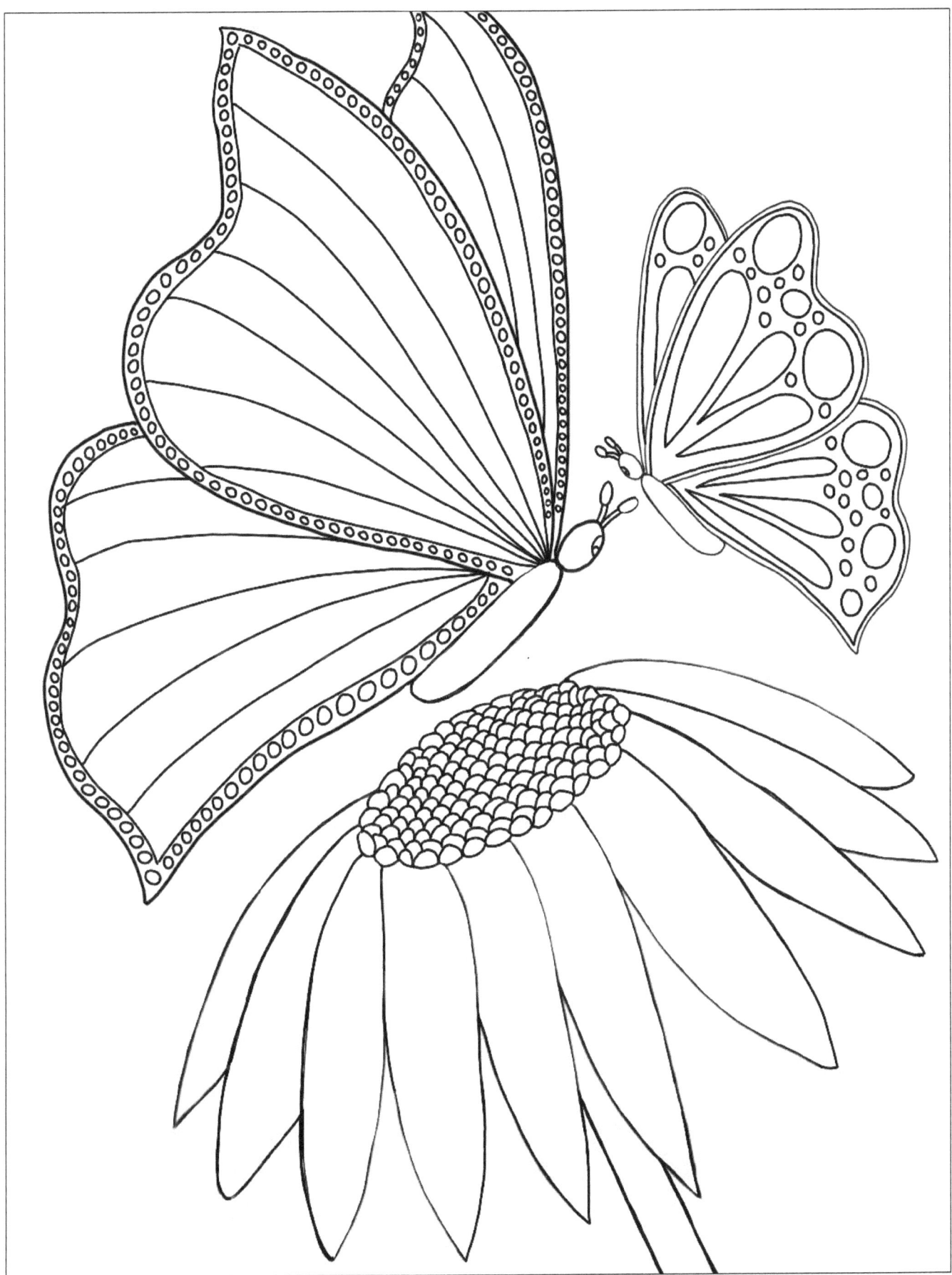

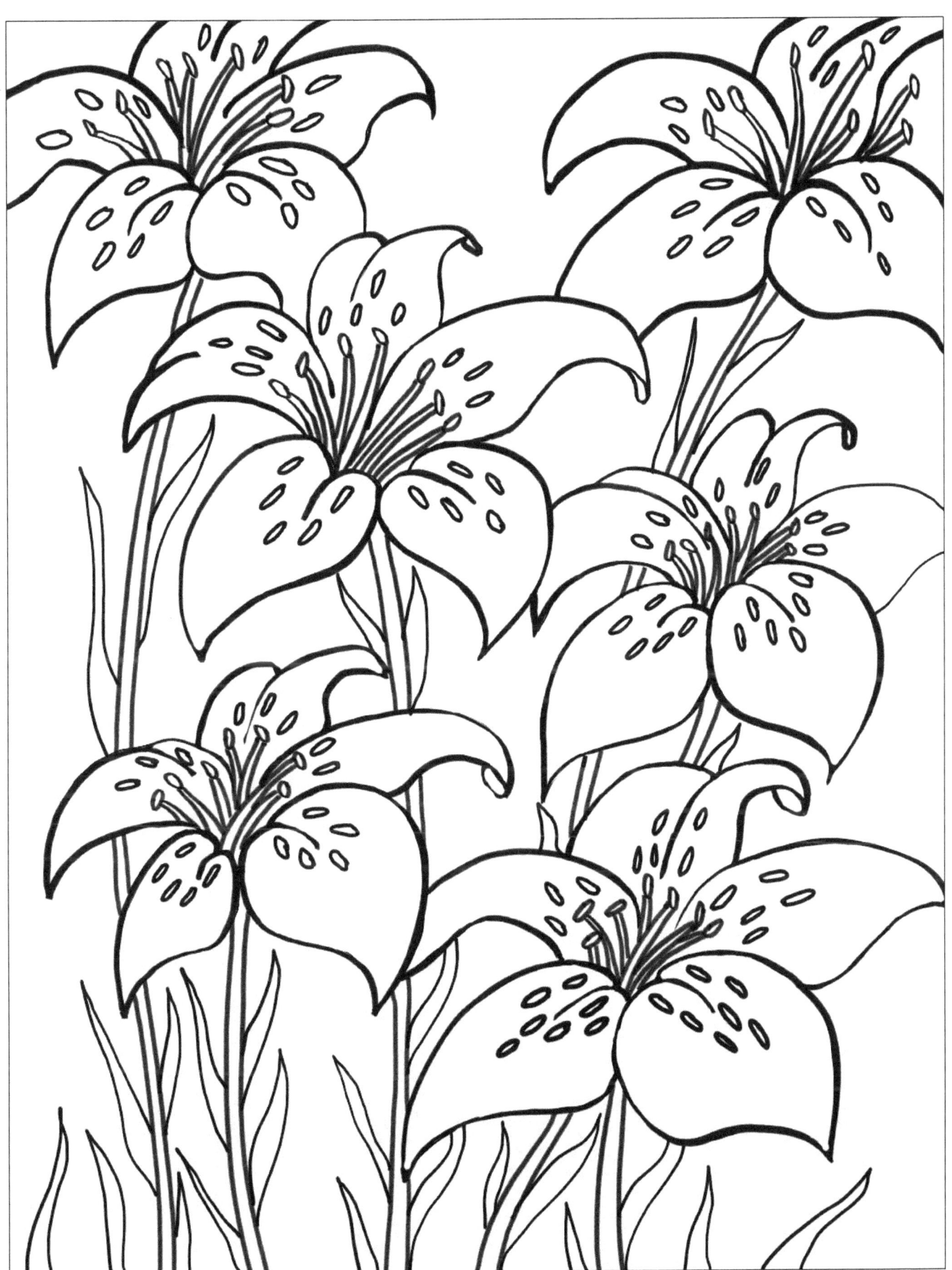

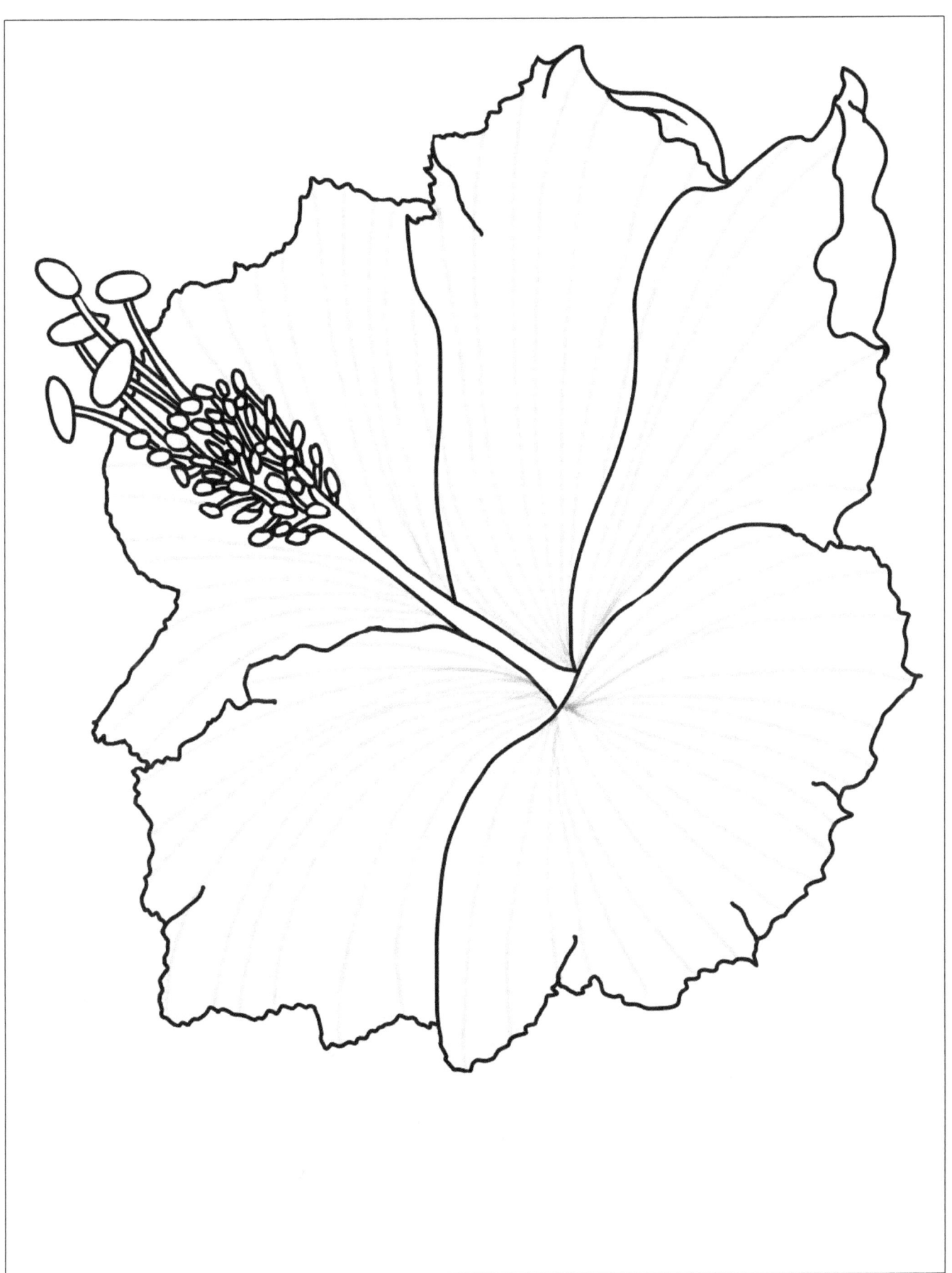

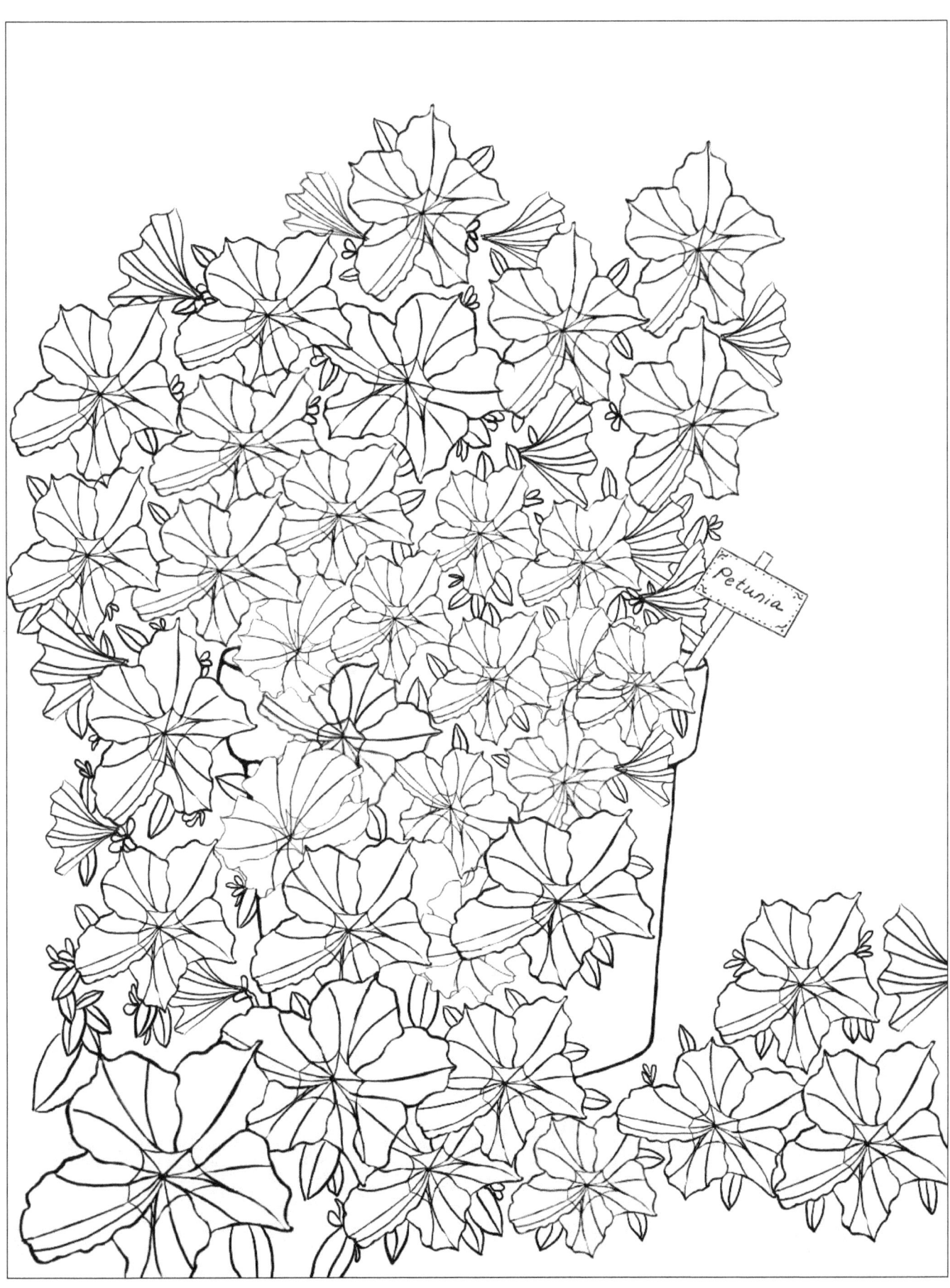

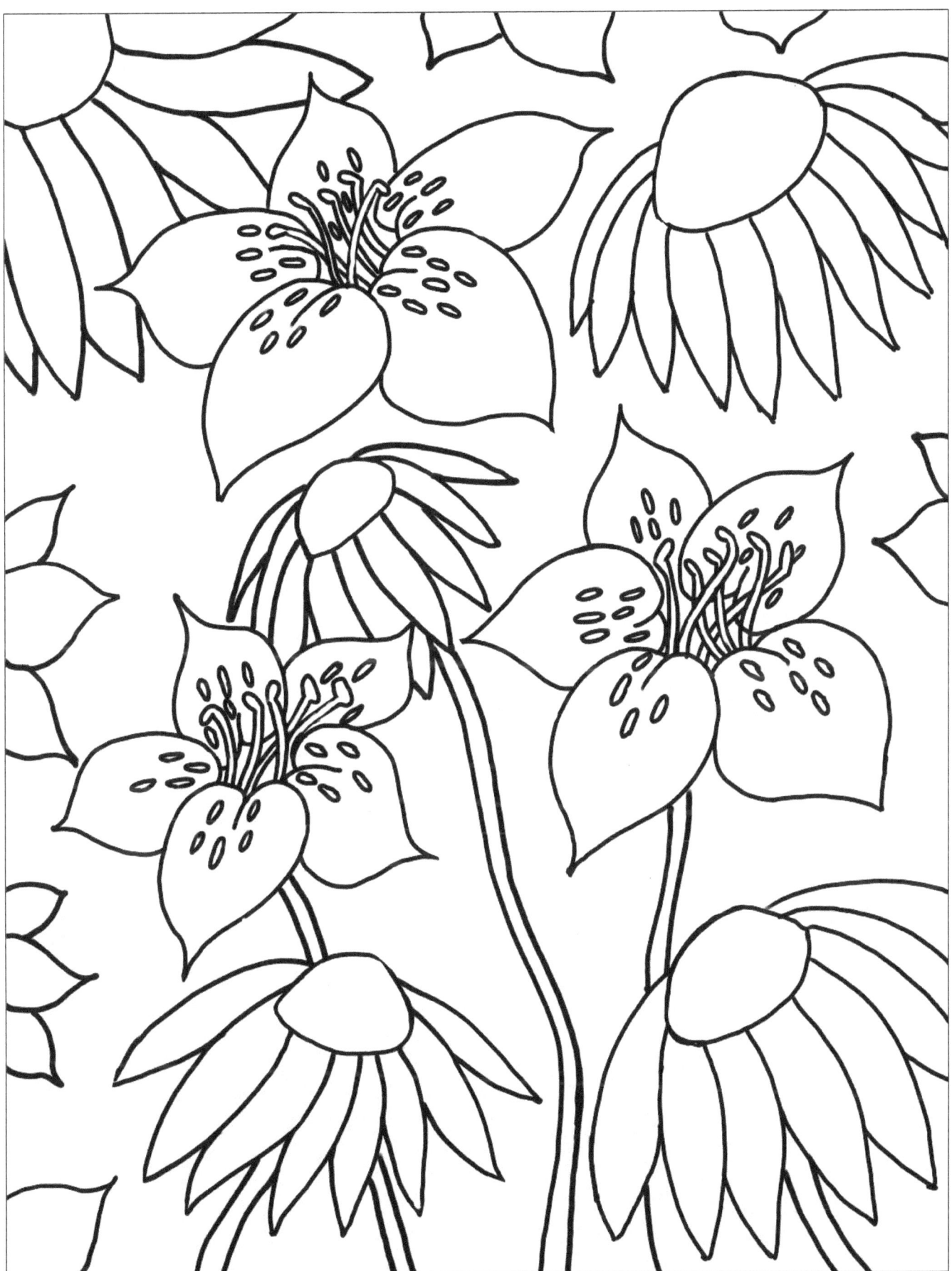

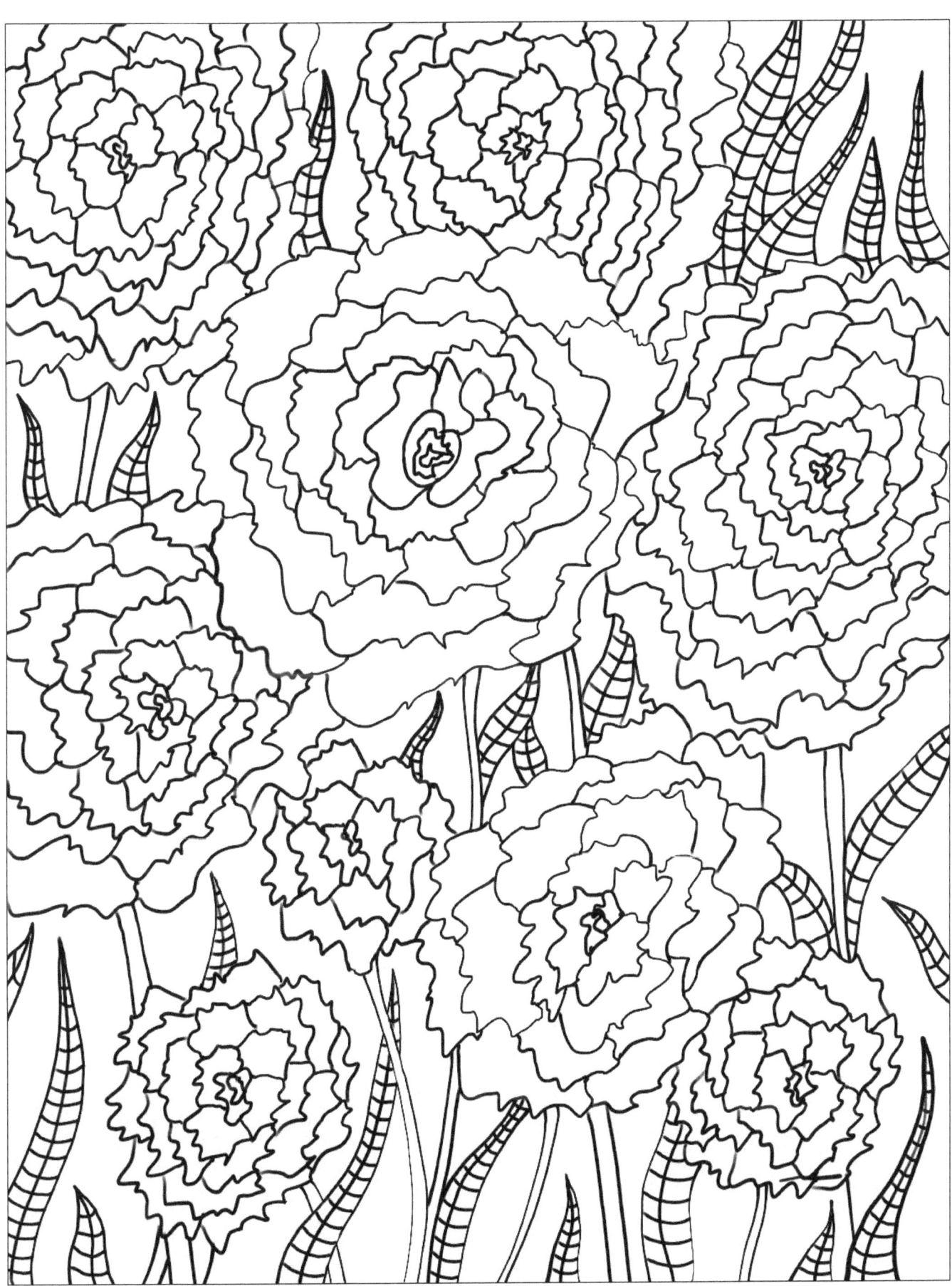

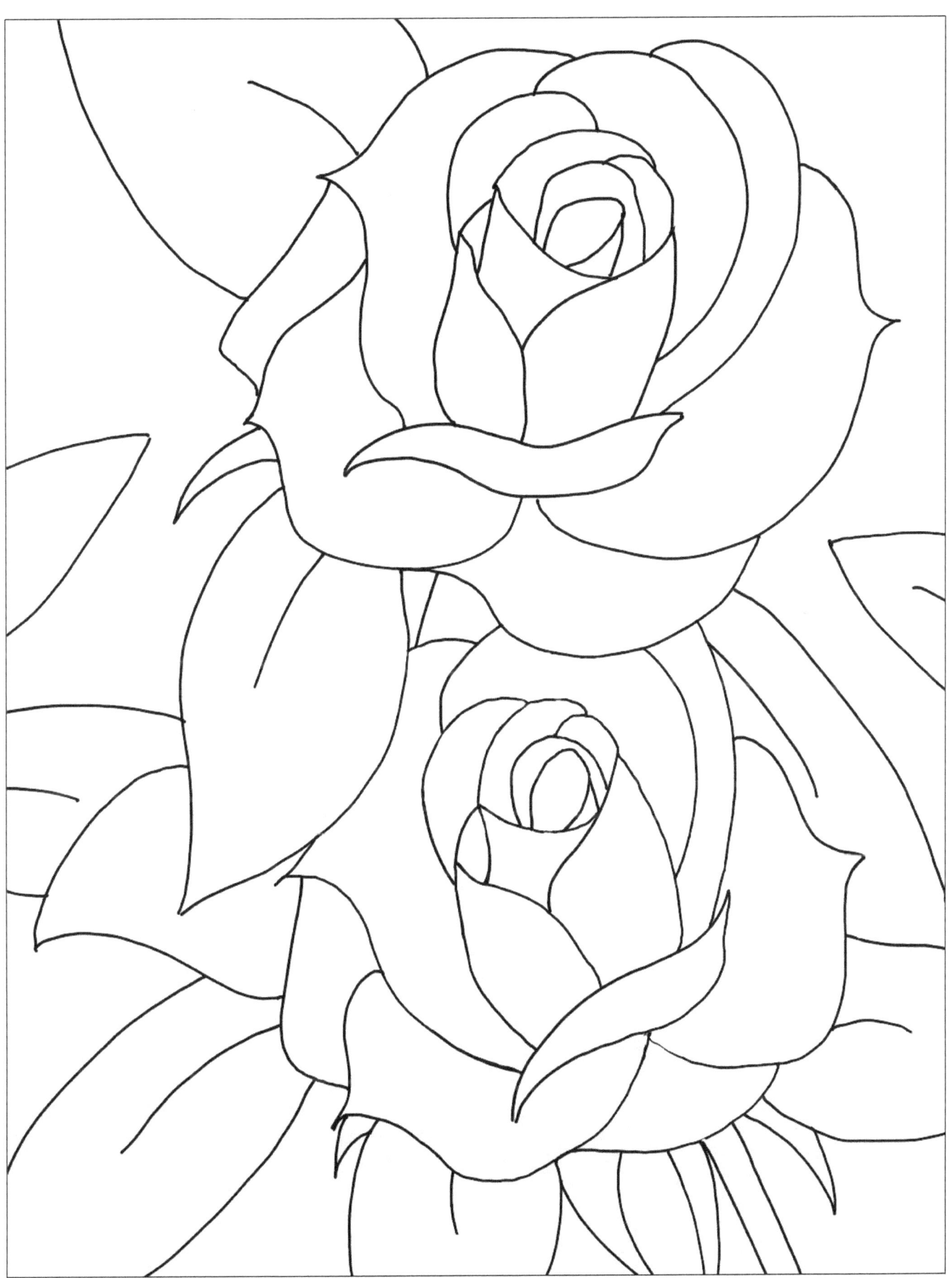

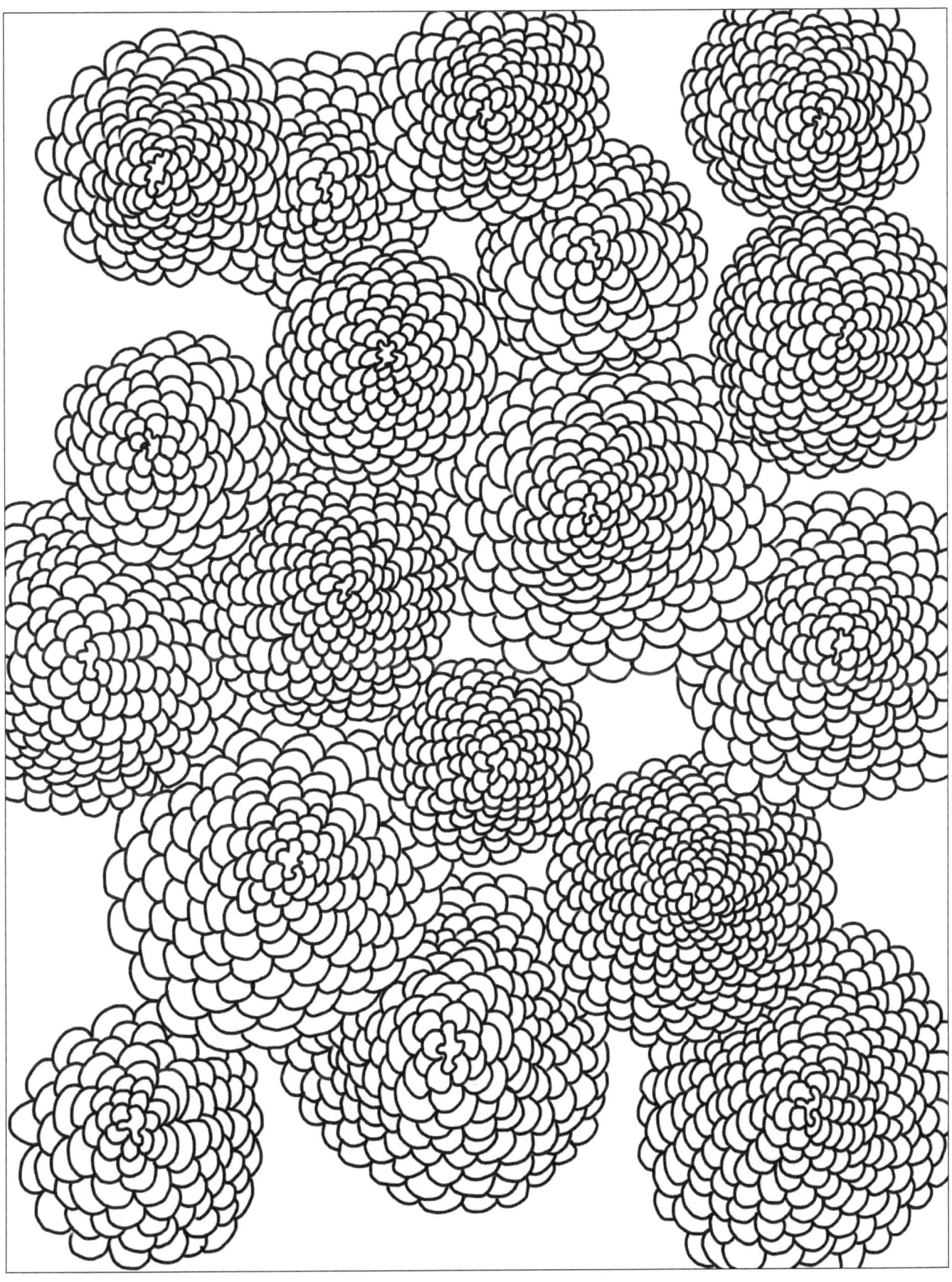

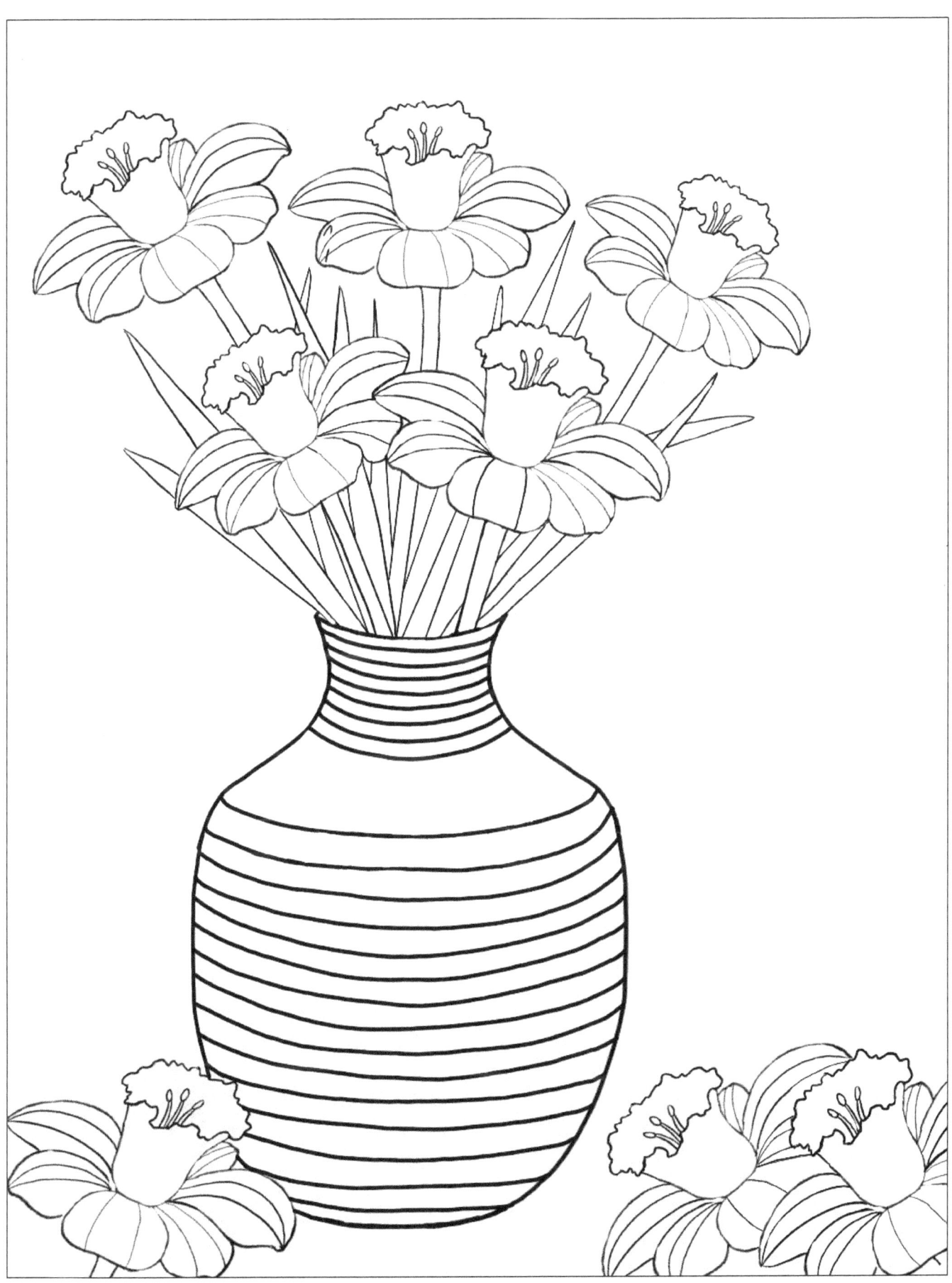

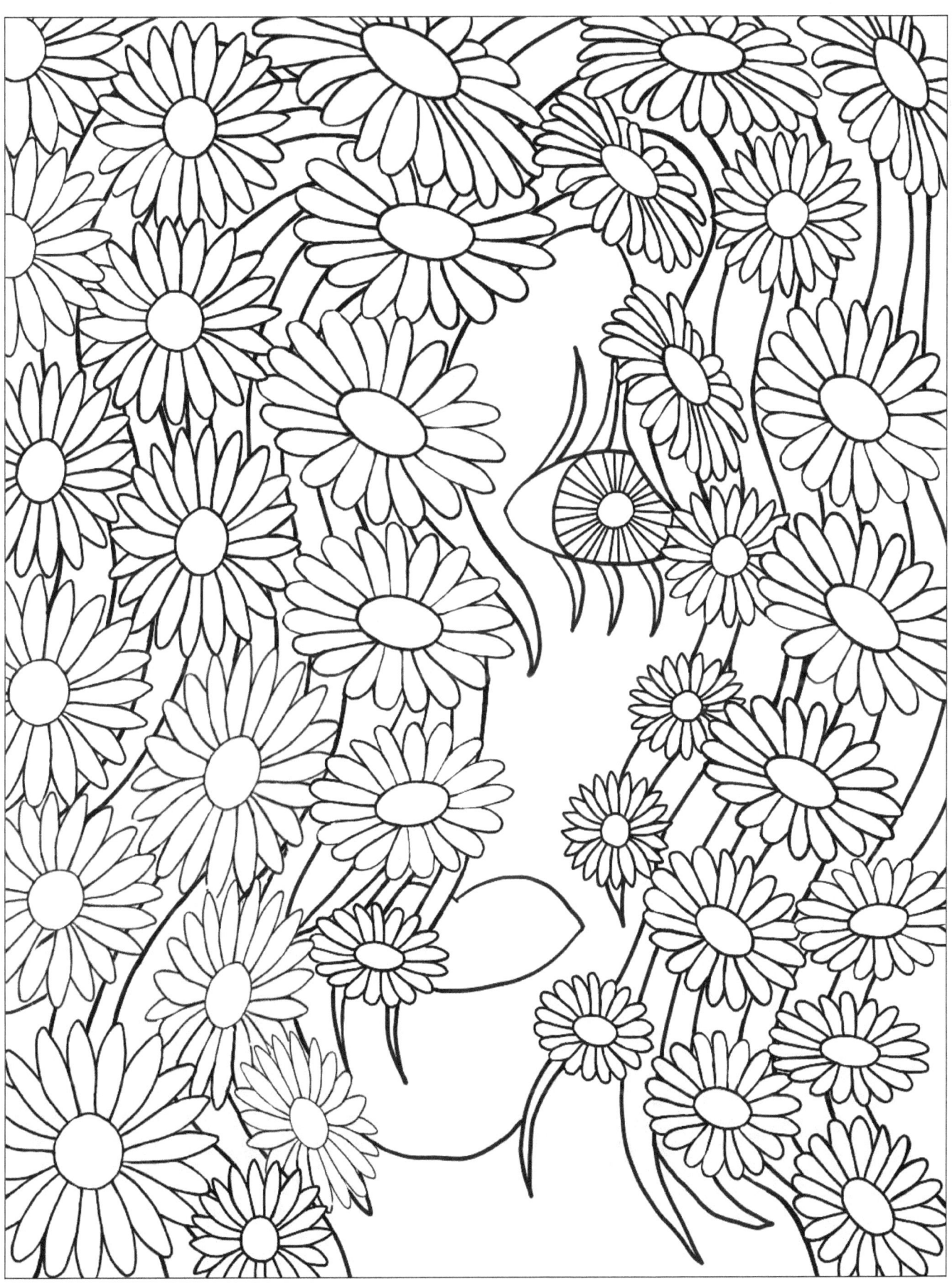

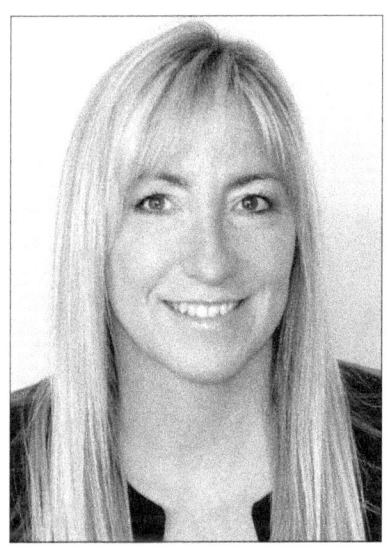

ABOUT THE AUTHOR

Cheryl Shireman is an author of many bestselling novels. In her spare time, she also enjoys writing books for children and creating coloring books for adults. She lives on a beautiful lake in the Midwest with her husband. Cheryl has three adult children and three adorable grandchildren. When she is not creating books, she enjoys mountain hiking, lake kayaking, and flower gardening. The first novel in her popular Cooper Moon series is now free as an ebook through most online vendors. You can find Cheryl and 2 Old 2 Color on Twitter, Facebook, and Instagram.

Visit the 2 Old 2 Color website for all of your adult coloring book needs. There you will find tips on coloring, featured adult coloring books, and reviews of a wide assortment of art supplies.

http://2old2color.com

www.ingramcontent.com/pod-product-compliance
Lightning Source LLC
Chambersburg PA
CBHW081212170526
45165CB00009B/2795